Staying Sane
When You're
Buying or Selling
YOUR HOME

Also available in the Staying Sane™ series

Staying Sane When Your Family Comes to Visit

Staying Sane When You're Dieting

Staying Sane When You're Quitting Smoking

Staying Sane When You're Planning Your Wedding

Staying Sane When You're Going Through Menopause

Staying Sane™
When You're
Buying or Selling
YOUR HOME

Pam Brodowsky
Evelyn Fazio

Da Capo
LIFE
LONG

A Member of the Perseus Books Group

Set in 11.5-point New Baskerville by the Perseus Books Group

Library of Congress Cataloging-in-Publication Data
Brodowsky, Pamela K.
    Staying sane when you're buying or selling your home / Pam Brodowsky, Evelyn Fazio.—1st Da Capo Press ed.
        p.   cm.—(Staying sane series)
    ISBN-13: 978-0-7382-1058-2 (pbk. : alk. paper)
    ISBN-10: 0-7382-1058-7 (pbk. : alk. paper)
    1. House buying—Psychological aspects.   2. House selling—Psychological aspects.   I. Fazio, Evelyn M.   II. Title.
HD1390.5.B76 2007
643'.12—dc22

                                                                                2006035576

Published by Da Capo Press
A member of the Perseus Books Group
www.dacapopress.com

Da Capo Press books are available at special discounts for bulk purchases in the U.S. by corporations, institutions, and other organizations. For more information, please contact the Special Markets Department at the Perseus Books Group, 11 Cambridge Center, Cambridge, MA 02142, or call (800) 255-1514 or (617) 252-5298, or email special.markets@perseusbooks.com.

1 2 3 4 5 6 7 8 9

To my father, who built hundreds of houses in
the 1950s and 1960s and who had hilarious
stories about it—and just about everything else.
—E. F.

To my husband, Edward, and our children,
Sarah and Jake, with love.
—P. B.

Contents

PART 1: STAYING SANE WHEN YOU'RE BUYING A HOME

2 When Realtors Are Helpful (or Not!) 49

3 When You're Buying a Newly Built House 81

4 When You're Buying a Condo or Co-op 109

PART 2: STAYING SANE WHEN YOU'RE SELLING A HOME

5 When Selling Is Boggling Your Mind 129

6 When You'll Try Anything to Unload It   177

About the
Staying Sane Series

The Staying Sane series is a collection of funny, irreverent, lighthearted, yet sassy, advice-laden books that are dedicated to finding the silver lining in the annoying, frustrating, or trying situations we all encounter every single day.

The Staying Sane series shows you how to look for, and find, the humor and enlightenment in nearly every situation—you only need to be open to seeing it. Let's face it: We all experience difficult or trying times in our lives, and that's precisely why we've developed the Staying Sane series.

We want you to know that we've been through all kinds of demented things ourselves (Oh, have we ever!), and we and our contributors plan to focus each volume on a specific topic to help you cope with some of the most trying, most typical—and most common—situations all of us face at one point or another as we try to get through life.

Unlike any other books, the Staying Sane series' intention is to shed light on—and bring laughter to—people who are caught up in a web of frustration and petty annoyances, and provide help, advice, and answers in every situation, while letting them know they are not the only ones who have suffered through these same trying, irritating episodes or situations. Since laughter is truly the best medicine, the Staying Sane series will help you get through whatever comes up with as few dents and bruises as possible, and with your family relationships and friendships still intact when all is said (or not) and done (or not!).

If you're like us, just hearing about other people's problems usually makes our own seem trivial by comparison, making us realize that things aren't really so bad. What's more, by reading about the scores of other people who've had the same or worse experience, we are able to find a more realistic perspective and regain our sense of proportion—all because we've been able to step back and see that things really could be much worse. And besides, misery loves company, doesn't it?!

Staying sane isn't as hard as you think. Keeping it together when all hell breaks loose is just part of life—something we have to do every single day if we're living on Planet Earth. But keep one thing in mind: there is always someone else out there who is also on the edge of losing it. We all lead complicated lives, but it doesn't mean we can't laugh at our problems—it can really help make them seem smaller and less overwhelming.

So, when things really seem to be getting out of hand and you just don't think you can take it anymore, pick up a copy of one of the Staying Sane titles. It may be just what you need to keep from going off the deep end. We'll be right there with you, helping you cope!

Let Us Know

We would be delighted to hear your reactions to the stories in this and all the other Staying Sane books. Please let us know which stories you liked best and how they related to your life.

We also would be very pleased if you'd send us your stories for upcoming volumes of the Staying Sane series. Is there a topic you'd like to see us cover? If so, let us know what it is you're looking for. We'll do our best to get a book into the works for you! Please write to us in care of our publisher.

We look forward to hearing from you!

Pam and Evelyn

About *Staying Sane When You're Buying or Selling Your Home*

What is it about buying or selling a home that brings out the lunatic in otherwise normal people? There's something about having strangers parade through the square footage you've called home (especially when we overhear their "honest" comments) that can leave many of us defensive and in no mood to sell the place after all! And, of course, there's that special stranger armed with a real estate license—the very definition of lunatic in some cases. On the flip side there's something about walking through other people's living quarters, often led by that same kind of license-toting stranger that can make one a little bit squeamish and shell-shocked.

What are you supposed to do when you step into a house and all you smell is cat pee in every single room? Or what about going into a house where everything you see—walls, carpet, shades, everything—is Pepto-Bismol pink, or some scary shade of purple? How do you see past all the clutter and chaos to find out what the place actually looks like? What about houses that don't have closets and half the plumbing isn't functioning? How do people live like that, and why would you want to buy from them?

And what if you've done everything you can to make your home sparkle and it doesn't ever satisfy your Realtor? After painting and redecorating, now she's saying you need to get the kitchen redone. But that'll only raise the asking price, and the real estate bubble might just be about to burst. Oh, what to do, what to do?

What about our friends the Realtors? Some of them are perfectly normal, but then there are the other kind: the loonies. The ones who think nothing of calling you at midnight to tell you to cut your price if you're selling, or else call you at 6:30 A.M. to tell you to increase your offer if you're buying. Then there's the type who try to push you into buying something you really don't want, then just won't leave you alone, no matter what you tell them. And those bizarre ones with five-inch fingernails so creepy that you're afraid to get into their cars with them to check out a property? Yep. We've heard about them all.

Those are just some of the kinds of things that can affect your sanity, to say the least. And then what? Then you're not staying sane—you'll no longer need to worry about real estate transactions because you'll have a special new home, with wire mesh windows, and nice soft padding all over the place!

So what should you do instead? We suggest you grab your copy of *Staying Sane When You're Buying or Selling Your Home*, sit down, put your feet up, and find out how our contributors coped. They all survived somehow, no matter how unlikely—even those poor, hapless buyers who lost three houses in a row to failed termite inspections; or the seller who couldn't shake a stalker Realtor; or the couple whose attempts to sell their house to a "friend" left them only partially sane because of a shady offer . . . that required the services of a "Goombah" to get them out of the deal! Yes, even they survived to laugh about it later, and you will too . . . in time.

So if you want to attempt to hang on to your sanity, you need to read the stories we've collected from all sorts of real estate veterans, whether they're buyers, sellers, Realtors, or neighbors, people who've remodeled and painted to get their house sold, or who've suffered through the actual building of their home and all the near catastrophes that entails. Misery loves company, so listen and learn!

Evelyn and Pam

PART 1: STAYING SANE WHEN YOU'RE BUYING A HOME

1

When House Hunting Challenges Your Sanity

Sanity Quiz

You've been preapproved by the bank for the home loan and are now in search of that special place to call your own. You've looked high and low and nothing you have found seems to fit all of your needs. The one you liked the best is one bedroom short and you really don't have the time to build a custom home.

Do you
A. sacrifice and do without the extra bedroom
B. take the house anyway, because it's a steal, and add on later
C. keep at your search until you find one that is exactly right
D. take the deal and force your guests to sleep on the sofa bed

However you answered that question, you'll learn new ways to cope from our experienced house-hunting veterans when you can't find exactly what you're looking for.

Termite Voodoo

John Janklov

OUR GOOD FRIENDS call my wife, Misty, and me "HPFs," short for historic preservation freaks. You see, for most of our lives, we have been in love with old, historic, city homes that were built when quality construction was important, and when detailed interiors were the rule, not the exception. Having majored in history in college, I take advantage of every historic neighborhood's tour of homes, both to explore old structures and to hear the stories of the many families who once called those houses home. And although Misty is an accountant, she was an architectural history major and has had a lifelong hobby of analyzing old homes' time periods and style.

As HPFs, Misty and I were out of place in an apartment built in 1989 with no redeeming architectural qualities. The irony had become painful to us and the brunt of jokes by many of our friends. We decided that the time had finally come to buy a home that matched our personalities and interests.

Jill, our new Realtor, whose territory centered on historic neighborhoods, first showed us a single-story classical Georgian-style home built in 1820. We immediately fell in love with the still-functioning central chimney and the grand high ceilings with original wood trim. As perfect as the home was, the setting was even better: an idyllic, shady, tree-lined street, with a lot surrounded by the original wrought-iron fence covered in decades-old ivy and clematis vines. Irrational, full of historic bliss, and emotionally attached to this home in minutes, Misty and I found the perfect spots for our collection of antique furniture and Victorian art.

An on-the-spot offer was immediately accepted by the seller. Not since our pot-smoking days in college had we been so high. We bounced off the ceilings as Jill explained an important condition of the buyer's contract—that the house must pass a thorough inspection. It was just a formality and we were so happy! Jill wasted no time suggesting a structural engineer who specialized in old house construction.

That inspection week was thrilling for us. We took photos of our new dream home's interior and critiqued paint swatches as we dreamed of just the right color for the parlor, the bedroom, and the dining area. Misty and I talked for hours about where and how to hang our antique chandelier, wrapped and in storage for years, that would finally have its proper place.

Then the engineers' report came back: To our shock and horror, our dream home was infested with termites, and the dollar amount required to fix the problem would be prohibitive. As you can imagine, terminating our conditional contract was highly disappointing for us, but Jill assured us that we would find another similar home that would make us just as happy. After all, there were at least a few dozen historic homes on the market in the area.

The next home we found was an Italianate style house, and we especially loved the narrow windows and original brick exterior. The home's low-pitched roof was supported by widely overhanging eaves with decorative brackets, and a seductive wraparound porch. Searching for any sign of termites, I scoured the porch's wood, which seemed to be in excellent condition, as did the windowsills, doorjambs, and wooden eaves. We fell head over heels again and signed another contract (and enjoyed another week of dreaming and planning) as we waited for the termite report—*foundation level infested.* Just like our second dream home's wood, the termites had also infested our hearts.

Twice bitten (by termites), we marched bravely with Jill up to a gingerbread-trimmed Queen Anne house. Featuring prominent bay windows, an interesting irregularly shaped roof, and original tiles on the mantles of three chimneys, we agreed that three had to be our charm. This glorious home was worth the wait, and we even ranked it as the best of what we'd seen so far. At 4,000 square feet, the home was huge, and the price was right.

"Could it be *too* right?" Misty asked as she pointed to the ground, wide eyed and open mouthed. To our horror, a dozen or so white cylinders were placed around the home's perimeter. Were those—oh heavens no! Yikes, they were indeed—*Termite traps!* Usually polite, Misty and I startled Jill by resorting to a most uncharacteristic string of gutter profanity. "At least this time there'll be no need for a professional inspection and waiting period," Jill consoled. This rationale didn't stop us from continued swearing, but we knew what she was saying was true.

That was it! We stopped looking for awhile to keep from completely losing our minds and giving up our dream. We'd invested too much emotional energy before the structural inspection came back. We knew that we needed comic relief and that it was time to take drastic action. So that night, Misty surprised me with a termite photo she'd found on the Internet. She enlarged the image and printed it out in full color. I then glued the termite onto a cardboard backing, a material perfect, I thought, for pins—voodoo pins.

While we waited for another call from Jill, we frequently took turns pushing pins into the termite. One by one, we tortured the bug that had tormented us over and over and over again, killing our hopes for historic-home living and squashing our dream-house dreams. We made up termite-voodoo chants and even a voodoo dance before and during our symbolic torture sessions. In a few days, we had a few dozen pins scattered over the head, wings, and legs, and we laughed and felt better with each prick. Then the phone rang again—it was Jill with a new house to show.

It was another Queen Anne. Beautiful. Ornate. Gingerbread trim galore! We tried to keep our composure as we walked the historic hallways and original stairs. This time, we came ready to fight as we pulled out our voodoo termite and pins. Asking Jill to do the honors, she found a perfect spot on one of his eyes, and then we enthusiastically signed another contract.

You know how this story ends: The inspection came back termite-negative, we moved in, hung the chandelier, placed our antiques, and are as happy as two HPFs can possibly be. Did our success have to do with termite-voodoo hexes or was the house already clean of pests? We'll never know!

When Your Seller Isn't Sane

Thomas Cook

WHEN I WAS a kid in the Midwest, my family lived in a seemingly endless series of tract homes. My parents liked them and sought them out. Nice enough, usually new, in fact, but dull, dull, dull.

As a young adult, I moved far way from these cookie-cutter suburban developments to the big city and lived happily for a decade and a half in rental apartments. My wife and I loved urban life, especially our sunny two-bedroom, two-bath, top-floor apartment with the glorious view. And the rent at that time was actually affordable.

Then disaster struck. Well, at least a big surprise. The real estate company that owned our apartment building left a thick prospectus in front of our door that told us the building was being converted to that peculiar institution, the cooperative, and it was time to either buy or move. A look through the book revealed that while the price of my apartment would be reasonable, my share of the underlying multimillion-dollar mortgage on the building was definitely not. When you added up all the fees and payments, my monthly payment was going to quadruple!

Our course was clear. It was time for my wife and me to purchase the single-family house we had been discussing for several years. Well, my wife had been discussing it while I nodded witlessly, visions of dull tract homes danced in my head. She definitely led the way.

Although we were by now flirting with middle age, neither of us had actually ever owned a house. I was unclear how to go about it. Neither of us knew exactly what we wanted. No matter, we had plenty of time. And this was, after all, the early 1980s and shockingly high interest rates were keeping most buyers out of the market. Properties were sitting empty for months or longer. The housing world was our oyster, so to speak, despite the rates.

Ignorant though I was, I had a short list of things I didn't want. I didn't want a tract house and I did not want a fixer-upper. I wanted a place in move-in condition. Janice, my wife, wanted a south-facing backyard so we could plant a garden. We both wanted a reasonable commute to our jobs. We drew a circle on a map. Janice consulted commuter bus schedules. It seemed so easy.

Mary, the real estate agent, was a great sport. Weekend after weekend we drove through the 'burbs, wandering from living room, to kitchen, to bedroom, to basement in dozens of homes. Nothing suited us, however. This one had a north-facing backyard. That one was too expensive. The commute was bad. The house was ugly. We learned a lot about house styles, layouts, and neighborhoods. The agent learned more about us than she probably cared to know.

One day, as we left another drab split-level on another tree-filled suburban street, Mary turned to us. "We have a little problem," she said. "I'm out of houses."

Well, she wasn't exactly out of houses, as it happened, but she was out of houses she had seen before and knew anything about. Wouldn't we like to go back to the office and look through the multiple-listing book (this was before the days of Internet listings) so we could see if there were any further prospects?

A half-hour flipping through the book gave us exactly four prospects in our price range that we had not already seen. The most promising, based on the tiny, faded black-and-white photo, was about $40,000 over our limit. As luck would have it, our agent dimly remembered that the price had been cut earlier that very week.

So we started with that one. A call to the listing agency eventually elicited the information that we could see the house in about an hour. We went to lunch, then headed towards the house.

As we pulled up to the curb, our eyes widened. A magnificent, stately, brick-and-stucco Colonial-style home rose before us, with a tall, imposing roof, and towering trees all around. Several stained-glass windows added highlights. Two mighty stone lions graced the front stairs. Birds chirped in the trees, and squirrels gamboled on the roof. My wife and I gasped. "Now this is more like it," I said. The agent beamed.

Mary rang the bell, the door opened, and a tall man appeared. He was sweating. His hair was bleached bright white with dark roots. He was holding a beer. A woman, apparently his wife, hovered in the background.

"I've cleaned up as best I could," he said, crossly. "We usually get more advance notice." He glared at me. Not a good start, I thought.

We entered. The smell of the feline litter box immediately assaulted us. Although familiar to us, as cat owners ourselves, this seemed considerably more powerful than what we were used to.

I looked around. Everything was a different shade of purple: the carpet, the walls, the furniture. Everything clashed with the area or item next to it. Where colors met, the effect was almost audible, screaming with disharmony. In the center of the nearly bare living room stood a portable bar, the type used in hotels during cocktail parties. A small dog barked frantically somewhere upstairs. What the hell was this place?

The owner looked at me with bleary eyes. "Want a beer?" he asked. I declined.

We wandered through the house with practiced efficiency, noting the cracked windowpanes, missing storm windows, the badly stained but otherwise new looking purple wall-to-wall carpets, and the peeling purple paint on the second floor woodwork (it was solid chestnut, I found out later). We peeked into the grease-covered kitchen (it was more or less white in color, a relief), noting the ancient almond-colored refrigerator, the 1950s countertop range, the fake "Kountry Kitchen" cabinets with their cracking veneer. We looked at the main bath and its fixtures of indeterminate age.

Then, a trip into the basement, where the smell of felines increased exponentially. The floors and walls were covered with the sheen of water. The basement had been recently hosed down. Not a good sign.

"No fixer-uppers," I mentally reminded myself. "And no catteries," I added.

We left, nodding and smiling at the frowning owner, now opening another beer. The wife had vanished. "It's a good deal," he growled. "Make us an offer."

We fled. I mentally crossed the house off the list. On the way out, I noticed that what I had taken to be squirrels were actually cats, bounding around on the roof.

In the agent's car, we reconnoitered. Janice and I both loved the way the house looked and, with some reservations, liked the layout. The house had exceptional character and style, with a particularly large yard. The house faced north, giving us the south-facing backyard for gardening. The street was utterly quiet and very attractive, with all types of dwellings: Colonials, Tudors, Federal-style, Foursquares, and Craftsman homes. Most were early twentieth-century vintage, from the 1910s to the late 1920s.

"You want to make an offer?" Mary asked. "They've really overpriced it. It's been on the market for months. We could lowball it and see if they'll go for it."

"No fixer-uppers," I said. "Disgusting kitchen," Janice added. "And the smell." We rolled our eyes. The agent laughed. We drove off.

"Too bad," I said. Without the smell, and the purple, and total lack of maintenance, the house was exactly what I wanted.

My wife agreed. "Just too many issues and too expensive," she said.

That evening, at home in our apartment, the phone rang. It was our agent. "The sellers of that first home we saw today are on my case," she said. "The guy complained to their agent that we're both wasting their time bringing around people who had no real interest. Can I make a really, really lowball offer in your name to get us off the hook?"

I demurred. "I really don't want to get into that," I said. "Is it really that big a deal?"

"Look, you saw what an oddball that guy was," she said. "He's screaming at his agent and she's on me about it. Just name a really crazy offer and you'll help us both."

Not wanting to get on the wrong side of my agent, I reluctantly quoted an absurdly low price.

An hour or so later, the phone rang again. Mary, the agent. "You are not going to believe this," she began. My eyebrows went up. Holding the phone, I turned and looked at my wife. My jaw slowly dropped. I knew what was coming.

"They took it," the agent said.

To this day, Janice and I have no clue whether or not we were set up. I personally think the agent was as surprised as we were; Janice thinks that the two agents worked up a story and managed to "work over" both buyer and seller (and who knows what they told the seller).

"I gotta think about this," I stammered. "Give us a day or two."

"I think I can give you only until tomorrow," the agent said.

So when tomorrow came, we took it. We signed the binder, and paid the deposit. Our attorney assured us that he could get us out of it if necessary.

The question was, how had I gotten myself into this? I suddenly had a binder on a home that violated my main rule. Sure, it was not a tract house, it had a garden-friendly backyard, it was within the commuter circle (both a bus and a train line), and fit our price range—after a reduction of roughly 33 percent of its value.

But it still had one glaring issue remaining: it was a fixer-upper. Big time. Could I handle this?

We proceeded. Our bank had preapproved us for a mortgage, but we needed their commitment on this specific property. My wife's parents generously offered additional private financing. My company would supply a small but welcome home loan at a favorable interest. Our savings account, such as it was, was sacrificed to the cause.

The owners arranged for a termite inspection (required by the state) and we hired a house inspector. The bank sent their appraiser. We notified our lawyer to prepare a contract that stipulated that the carpet would be removed and no cats and dogs left behind. We discovered there were nine cats and two dogs living there, including at least two cats that lived on the roof.

The house inspector was a gem. Braving the pet smells, he and I climbed and crawled through the nooks and crannies of the house and discovered the extent of the repairs needed. As later events proved, he spotted virtually all the potential problems. His rough estimate of possible repair costs was fairly close.

We knew by now that getting the owners to pay for any repairs was out of the question, given the vastly reduced price and the obviously sad state of their finances. Still, having a good, thorough home inspection was well worth it and helped us know what we were getting into.

The appraiser and the termite inspectors were a different story. Both were deeply offended by the cat smells and the odd behavior and lifestyle of the current owners. They decided to take it out on us.

The appraiser listed every flaw he could find and sent it to the bank. I could not believe the list. One bedroom needed a closet. That was fair, as the existing closet had been sacrificed to a crude, home-handyman bathroom extension at some point in the life of the house. But two tiny holes in a door, caused by termites or carpenter ants treated years before? A second closet in a homeowner-built attic "room" that we intended to turn back into an empty attic anyway?

The bank was as implacable as it was unreasonable. They insisted that in order to sign off on our loan, we would have to agree to build a new closet and fill the termite holes once we'd taken ownership of the house. As instructed, we put several thousand dollars into an escrow account for this purpose; the bank would give us this money back for the necessary repairs once we'd closed on the house.

It was as if the bank was working against us, daring us to buy the house despite the obstacles they threw in front of us. *We'll make it as hard as we can,* they seemed to say, *and if you can stand it, we'll reward you by lending you money at 16 percent.*

The stack of bank forms to fill out we could live with. The stream of petty fees we could stomach. It was when they lost all the papers and tried to bill us for the fees a second time around that my wife and I started to get annoyed. Then when they came up with yet another set of forms, different from the first forms, we began to get really irritated.

The origin of the next seemingly insurmountable problem was the termite man. In our state, the homeowner arranges for the termite inspection. Something we don't have to worry about, we thought. Wrong!

While the original owners lived in the home, their practice was to squirt a hose around the basement instead of sweeping the floor. Odd, yes, lazy, yes, but not exactly destructive. This meant that the concrete floors and walls were sometimes slightly damp. Like when the termite man came.

So the termite extermination report to the bank found the house to be currently free of termites. It stated that he had given the house a full termite prevention treatment and provided a guarantee. But it gratuitously reported that the house was infested with cats and that the basement walls were damp.

The bank, in their wisdom, decided that the basement needed to be waterproofed. No word on the cats.

By now my wife and I were nearing bank bureaucracy burnout. I called the mortgage officer. Water wasn't leaking into the basement, I pointed out through clenched teeth. It was sprayed from a hose. No hose, no water, no problem.

"Sorry," I was told. "It says on the report that the walls are damp."

I called the exterminator. He would not budge. He made several comments about the cats and about the owners. I made comments about his lack of expertise on wet walls. He said that the law required him to report wet walls. I asked him if he had a license to practice law. We had words. He hung up.

I phoned the vice president of the bank. No, he couldn't interfere with the mortgage process. Besides, the walls were damp. It said so on the termite report.

"Is the termite inspector an expert on damp walls?" I asked. Well, no. But if it's on the report, the bank needed the walls waterproofed.

I lost it. Despite all the work I had put into trying to buy this house, I couldn't take any more. "Well," I said to the bank officer, heedlessly throwing a month of filling out forms to the winds, "I'm not planning to waterproof the ****ing basement, not even if Noah's flood is predicted again. I guess we'll just have to forget about the ****ing mortgage and allow the ****ing deal to fall through."

Sometimes, gentle reader, going for the long ball pays off. There was a silence on the other end for a brief second. The man at the bank cleared his throat. Static rattled the phone line.

"Oh, let's not be hasty," he said. "I think we can work this out."

Clouds parted. Light flooded the world. Bankers, I discovered, are slaves to pieces of paper. If it says "damp" on the report, then the walls are, ipso facto, damp. And if you don't like what the report says, the solution is simple: just get another report. The answer to the waterproofing problem had revealed itself: have a second termite inspection.

I called our lawyer and he called the exterminator he had used in countless home inspections. We removed the report from the earlier inspection, retaining the treatment contract and the guarantee for the bank. "Don't mention basement walls," the lawyer said to the exterminator. Problem solved.

Meanwhile, another surreal piece of insanity was brewing. During the house inspection, I had noticed several odd situations inside the house. The stone lions on the front steps, a quirky, attractive feature of the house, had disappeared. All the storm windows in the house were stacked neatly next to the front door—in summertime. Several overhead lights and chandeliers were missing, leaving bare wires in their place. Almost all the furniture in the house was gone—only two beds, a few chairs, an end table, a TV, and a dinette table remained.

"Did you move your furniture already?" I asked the owner's wife. "Oh, no, we just had a big yard sale," she replied.

Call me paranoid, but I wondered what other parts of the house had been sold!

I called our lawyer, who promised to deal with it. Foolishly, I didn't ask how. Unbeknownst to me, he simply sent a threatening lawyer letter warning the sellers that if they sold any parts of the house we would take legal action.

This triggered what can only be described as a drunken, threatening, screaming phone call around midnight a few days later. Blindsided, I stammered a little, while listening to a five-minute tirade that cannot be effectively rendered in a family-oriented book. I was torn between apologizing for the letter, which, mild though it was, was truly overkill, and worrying about having the faucets, sinks, crystal doorknobs, and stained glass sold for two bucks apiece in the front yard.

We finally agreed that the owner was certainly not a crook, that he would not sell off any more light fixtures, and that I would give up on the stone lions. We further agreed that the owner would sleep it off and could call me in the morning. He never did.

So we lost the lions (but a decade later, we replaced them with much nicer ones). We traded the already sold chandeliers, which we didn't like anyway, for the refrigerator, which we also didn't like but that served us for another twelve years. The storm windows stayed—they were never for sale, just stacked in an odd place.

At the closing, both owners appeared, dressed neatly for the first time. Their attorney hustled in. "Morning Willie," he said to the husband. "Sober this morning?" Willie chuckled. The wife looked around nervously.

We then proceeded to sign numerous papers, pay still more fees, and pass around large cashier's checks. In turn, the owners paid off a substantial lien on the house's recently replaced furnace, a surprise to us.

We drove back to our new house, intent on making sure the cats had been removed. We found Willie and his wife packing the last of their possessions into a small rented van. One cat remained, but they promised to return for her. "We can't leave Winkie behind," he said, in the first real sign of compassion I had heard from him.

Two days later Willie returned for Winkie. My wife and I were stripping wallpaper. An architect was measuring the second floor to plan for rebuilding it in a different configuration. The former owners found Winkie, enticed her into a cat carrier, and left, never to be seen again.

As agreed with the bank, we had a contractor build the requisite closets and fill several tiny termite holes with plastic wood to pass the second appraisal and get our escrow money back. Even the second appraisal guy was baffled at the zeal of the earlier one. After the bank was satisfied, we then tore down both closets to remodel the second floor and put insulation in the attic!

We had decided to stay in our apartment for six months while the renovations took place, a wise decision, as it turned out. My wife and I spent six exhausting months stripping old paint, repainting, cleaning, and caulking some parts of the house while the construction crew completed the more extensive renovations in other parts.

The strong cat and dog smells, despite what everyone tells you, became nothing but a memory. All it took was a reasonably thorough basement cleaning and refinishing all the wood floors.

Twenty-five years later, we are still in the house, now much changed and improved after two additional interior remodeling projects. The outside, except for a color change of the trim, remains nearly as it was that first day we drove up. Neighborhood children stop by to ride on our replacement lions, which we have named Edgar and Clyde after our favorite law enforcement officials. Janice's garden has become a neighborhood showplace in the spring. Everybody says what a nice house it is. It has increased in value more than 400 percent.

We're just about ready to move again.

SURVIVAL HINTS

1. When house hunting, sometimes you have to look past strange owners and weird behavior.
2. Don't be thrown by odd decor and bizarre colors. A coat of paint can make a huge difference.
3. Sometimes getting a second inspection can save the day, so don't give up too soon.

All of Murphy's Laws

Faun Nikoy

IT IS PROBABLY a rite of passage or karma, but everyone seems to live through buying at least one house from hell, with all the trimmings. On the day that I first met mine, I was at work.

That fateful Friday afternoon, I returned to my humble, privacy-defying cubicle somewhere in the dark bowels of a major corporation, just after the latest "brainstorming strategy charting session." The telephone rang as if on cue. It was my wife. "Honey! I have great news! We're buying a house! Meet me in forty-five minutes at the mall." And then phone went dead. I learned a long time ago that "great news" for my wife means either a ruined weekend, a missed round of golf, or some other calamity for me.

After the usual crawl-and-sit rush-hour traffic—surviving the hundreds of drivers desperate to squeeze into the six-foot space between me and the vehicle ahead—I made it to the mall. My wife was talking enthusiastically to a stern, grim-looking lady, who was as animated as a marble tombstone and reminded me of my high school principal. She was the listing Realtor of some high-priced property in an exclusive, prestigious neighborhood, so naturally my wife was beside herself with excitement to be speaking with her.

I have never figured out why is it so important to live within a specific zip code when there are lots of comparable properties just two streets away at a better price. And I have never figured out why people want to live in the center of a big city. It must involve serious and permanent damage to their self-esteem to do otherwise. It certainly holds no appeal for me. But my wife is another story.

So first we sat with the lady at a corner table in the food court of the mall, with a generous serving of quite expensive sushi. The lady opened her attaché case and pulled out some ominous-looking questionnaires full of curious diagrams, circles, questions, and squares. Having sensed my anxiety, she assured me that after the allotted time was up, she would have a better idea of the kind of house that fit our personality and lifestyle. I am a survivor of multiple corporate-personality tests, with endless variations on whether I was a problem child at school, or whether I ever wanted to run away from home, but a test to determine my fit with a house? In my naïveté I thought we would be talking finances, expenses . . . and debt!

After we finished answering her questions, the Realtor pulled out a fancy cell phone and rolled it over the questionnaires. It was some sort of scanner that allowed her company to instantly know our marketing personality profile, and all of our information was secured and triple encrypted on their corporate server. Evidently, we must have aced the test, as we were invited to follow the Realtor to a remote, tree-lined suburb. Modest houses, separated by at least a quarter-mile-long driveway from the main road, started at about ten times my salary, while bigger houses suggested a sizeable full-time domestic staff to keep up with the flower gardens, the trees, and everything else.

We stopped at a corner-lit house and the Realtor took another curious-looking gizmo from her vest pocket. After some clicking, the lockbox on the door miraculously opened and we went in. We entered a large, barracks-sized kitchen. The house had rooms big enough to hold a bachelor party in each.

My wife started firing meaningful questions about utility bills, homeowner fees, neighbors, and schools at a speed to make any self-respecting sports commentator ashamed. The Realtor kept talking in a well-rehearsed, robotlike voice. After about a quarter of an hour, and my wife having committed the details of the conversation to her PDA, the Realtor looked at me over the rim of her tortoiseshell glasses: "I have several other houses in this area. I suggest we visit all of them so you can make up your mind."

For the next several weekends, we drove around that and several similar neighborhoods, my wife furiously scribbling on her PDA and bringing color diagrams, and the Realtor talking in her patented, otherworldly voice. At this point I was ready to sign anything, buy anything, just to get it over with, despite being not even close to making up my mind. After so many houses, and hours and hours of looking at properties, my head was spinning, whereas my wife's excitement was reaching the stratosphere.

Finally the house viewing ended when my wife, having filled a thick binder with pictures of houses, diagrams, comparisons, and marketing analyses worthy of a major promotion department, announced: "Honey, this is it! I have finally found the house of our dreams. This house will no doubt suit your important position in the company and, once we start entertaining, you may even get promoted!"

We signed the contract and thus began my hell on earth. The Realtor had a mortgage-broker friend, so as a courtesy we spent the next several weeks chasing bank statements, employment records, confirmations, and verifications of every imaginable kind, doing his job. With my luck, several companies that I'd worked for had just fallen off the face of the earth. The same with our banks—by way of mergers and acquisitions or just bad business luck. As if this were not enough, I had to write many pages of explanations as to why I left such and such company, where I had been making more than at my current job. To top it all off, I had to answer in detail whether I had had anything to do with the untimely demise of several former companies!

My wife kept a daily status report on who said what and when, and what new words we learned that day. Of course, the money that we had for a down payment was not enough, so we had to get a letter from a relative who was willing to part with a nice chunk for us as a gift. Then it turned out that the money had to be "seasoned," which made my skin crawl. As one who considers himself a great chef, at least in his own mind, and has some idea of how to season various meats, I was baffled by the concept of seasoning money: well cooked, medium, or raw? I wondered how exactly one seasons one's money. As it turned out, it just had to stay quietly in the bank for a while.

Then the mortgage broker called me in the middle of the night to tell me that he had found a lender who did not need seasoned money. Of course there was also bad news—the woman who was handling our file got married on a whim and took off with a huge pile of files, so naturally my documents were gone as well. Before I collapsed from disbelief, my wife managed to dig up copies of all the documents, so we decided to drop them off to her replacement mortgage clerk in the morning.

The next day, after several wrong turns into unmarked one-way streets, I finally made it to the broker.

The office was in the middle of a paper cyclone, several fax machines spitting reams of paper onto the floor, joined by some elderly printers. I waited fifteen minutes, then, after meeting not a soul, I ventured through a door, where I heard loud yelling and a choice of four-letter words.

There was a youngish creature of indeterminate sex whose bright orange and sky-blue hair was tied up in a knot with rubber bands and paper clips, revealing a nice green barcode number tattooed on the back of his/her neck. There was enough metal in the ears, eyebrows, and mouth to set off an entire airport full of security screening devices. The individual was juggling several heavy files in manicured hands while cradling a phone receiver on one shoulder.

Seeing me, the person waved me in and continued yelling into the receiver: "What do you mean you can't calculate one point of this loan—and you are a title company? Lord have mercy!" Then the being slammed the phone and picked it up again: "The appraiser missed a whole bedroom? And his math does not add up! Oh, my soul!"

He finally looked at me: "Hi! I am Jake and I work on your loan. I have been at this job for two weeks and I already know more about it than all the big name Realtors, appraisers, and title companies. They are so full of themselves; it cracks me up to point out their stupid mistakes. Don't worry; you will close three days from today. You know what, when money talks, everybody gets their act together!"

And it came to pass that three days later, a miracle happened. Jake managed somehow to clean up all the messes made by all his predecessors, and then my wife and I, accompanied by the patrician Realtor, sat at the long mahogany table for the closing. At last it was finally my turn, and we signed and signed, seemingly in slow motion, until we finally owned our house!

SURVIVAL HINTS

1. Keep copies of all your paperwork—things often get lost along the way, and it's much easier when you have copies.
2. Don't judge brokers or Realtors by their appearance. Some of the oddest turn out to be the best!

A Foot in the Door to Homeownership

Bob Toriello

OWNING A HOME is the American dream, and this is
the story of our personal version of that dream. My wife
and I had been living in a three-bedroom, two-bath rental
house for four years. We often talked about how much we
enjoyed living there. It was close to my job as a title
searcher, and there was a shopping center just minutes
away. We had settled in, and loved the beautiful courtyard-
atrium entrance. My wife, an aspiring interior decorator,
had put her own, distinctive stamp on the place, and was
reluctant to consider moving.

After discussing all our options, and whether we
could afford it, we decided to approach our landlady

and ask if she would consider selling the house to us. She and her husband had bought the house in the 1950s and had raised their children in it. Her husband had passed away some years earlier, and she had moved to a condominium. She then rented out the house; we were only the second family to rent it.

The previous renters did not take care of the place, but when my wife found the house she immediately fell in love with it. Now, four years later, we were ready to take the next step towards homeownership.

Our landlady was an elderly woman who lived in the next town. She had various health problems, especially asthma. That, however, did not stop her from traveling frequently to see her family and friends. Little did we know that her health problems would soon play a sig-nificant part in our ability to realize our dream of homeownership.

After the holidays, one Saturday when our rent was due, we decided to pay our landlady a visit and discuss the possibility of buying the house. We were well pre-pared and presented her with our plan to purchase her house. To our surprise, she was very receptive to our offer, and told us she had been thinking about selling. The house was beginning to be a burden for her. Her health problems were making it difficult to manage her day-to-day responsibilities, and she was planning to put it on the market. She was thrilled that we wanted it; it would be one less thing she would have to think about.

She bragged about how she did not have to put much money into the house for repairs. Partly this was because I was handy around the house and was able to fix the little things that needed doing. But little did she know that the roof leaked a bit, and that the electricity and plumbing were beginning to show their age and would need a lot of work.

She agreed to give us first crack at buying the house. We were ecstatic. We tried to contain our excitement as we skipped down the path to our car. On Monday we would begin the arduous process of finding a bank that would give us a mortgage. Our dream was in sight! But in reality, it was far in the distance.

Bank after bank refused to lend us the money. Our credit wasn't perfect, and we began to see our dream slipping away. Then a friend told us about mortgage brokers who worked with companies who were able to help financially challenged couples like us. We had tried going through the front door, but now the side door was beginning to open, and in we stepped. But the process dragged on for months, and unbeknownst to us, our landlady's health had taken a turn for the worse.

We finally found a small mortgage brokerage run by a husband and wife team who found us financing. The payments were a lot more than we had budgeted for, but we thought we could swing it. Things were falling into place at last!

But in June we were dealt another blow. Sadly, we learned that our landlady had passed away and had left the house to her son, in trust for his two daughters. He lived in the northern part of the state. We had met him only once, years ago. Now we were faced with dealing with a stranger, rather than our kindly landlady. Soon the son sent us a letter, which stated in part that if we wanted to buy the house, we could do so only under his terms, which he set forth in the letter. There were to be no further negotiations.

We arranged for home and termite inspection reports, and through my title company were able to find out the comparable home-sale prices in the area. There were plenty of problems with the house, and this would affect the price as well as the mortgage. We sent the new owner our proposal, and, backed by the inspection reports, offered $20,000 less than his asking price. That must not have gone over well, because the following week a Realtor put a For Sale sign on our front lawn. We were devastated. Our dream of buying the house had turned into a nightmare; now we would have to move.

But being optimistic people, we persevered. We knew that when one door closes, another opens, and we were determined to find that door. There were new homes being built on the north end of town. The subdivision was only ten minutes away. One day after work I picked up my wife and we drove out to inspect the models. The first three-bedroom model home we walked into was absolutely perfect for us! This was the one we wanted. Our furniture would fit exactly into the floor plan, and we loved the design and layout of the kitchen and great room. We went back to the sales trailer to talk to a salesperson.

Nervously, we walked up the stairs. The smiling saleslady welcomed us at the front door. Then, little over an hour after seeing the model house, we were signing papers to buy our brand new home! It couldn't have been easier, and it literally fell into our laps.

After having gone through the entire arduous process of trying to find a mortgage and dealing with all the setbacks and new landlord with our rental house, which was in worse condition than we realized, and after all manner of roadblocks every step of the way, we should have realized that it just wasn't meant to be, because sometimes when things are that difficult, it's as if someone is trying to tell you something!

When that first house fell through we were upset, but we were determined not to be denied our dream. And then we found our dream house, and the process flowed as easily as possible. Buying our house taught us that sometimes when one door closes, it's just an indication that somewhere a much nicer door is waiting to open!

SURVIVAL HINTS

1. Don't be thrown when unexpected roadblocks turn up in your quest to buy a home.
2. Don't give up if you don't get what you want the first time around—sometimes something much better is waiting for you!
3. Be patient when searching for your new home. It can take longer than you expect.

Spring in the Air

Ginny Chandoha

FOR MORE THAN a decade we'd dreamed of fleeing the metropolis. In 1999, my husband was transferred by his company from New York to northern New Hampshire. It was a welcomed transfer as we had been planning to retire and move to the quiet mountains of New England at some future time anyway. Why not be paid to go there?

Buying a house in northern New Hampshire is a real eye-opener, especially when you're accustomed to living in a metropolitan area regimented by rules and regulations. In the New York area, there are strict building codes, building inspections, certificates of occupancy, and a Realtor is nothing more than a house key. Once an offer on a house has been accepted, the lawyers step in to slug it out. The housing market is so tight, there are often bidding wars on a single property. We were unprepared for, but refreshed by, the laid-back, handshake-is-good-enough atmosphere of home buying in the North Country.

We met with Mona, the broker for the area's Century 21 chain. She was very professional, but dressed casually, unlike the suited agents we were accustomed to. She asked all the right questions, trying to get an idea of what we were looking for. Having spent the last ten years converting our ranch-style home into a contemporary, naturally I assumed that that would be the style we'd be interested in. Large, airy rooms, an open floor plan, but most importantly, a home up in the mountains. After having lived in a high-density area for a quarter of a century, we wanted peace and quiet. I always said I didn't want to have to hear or see another living human being unless I chose to. However, I was surprised when my husband said we'd look at any style house, and that he was also interested in houses with a barn that he could convert into a woodworking studio. Northern New Hampshire being rural farm country, that criterion would certainly narrow things down! NOT!

Since we'd sold our house in New York for more money than we'd ever imagined, buying a new home in a languishing market would not be a financial difficulty. Mona had several properties to show us right away, and we eagerly looked forward to viewing one magnificent property after another.

First up was an old farmhouse down a winding country road. We soon learned that only the main roads were paved, and all of the country roads were dirt, which turned to mud in spring. The farmhouse was very tired and run-down. We drove past the huge pasture that smelled like your head was stuck right in the cow's behind. The scent assailed the nostrils of the novice to the area, but apparently was odorless to the lifetime inhabitants. It was an odor we dubbed "spring in the air."

The farmhouse obviously hadn't had any repairs in a very long time, but it had a big barn. My husband took one look at the barn, complete with poured concrete stalls and animal muck, not to mention the small mountain of decaying manure that had been bulldozed down the hill behind the barn and he told Mona this was not what we'd envisioned. It would take a lot of cement to make the floor flat and smooth, and it would be impossible to get the manure stench out of the wood. A couple more visits to farms and Mona quickly realized my husband really didn't want an actual barn, just a building that looked like one. We, in turn, quickly realized that we didn't want to live anywhere on or near a farm because field fertilization can bring tears to your eyes.

The next memorable place was a ranch-style home in reasonable condition, with a nice view of the mountains and a new gambrel-roofed outbuilding that made my husband's eyes light up. However, the house would need renovation to open up some rooms and finish another,

and while the view was nice, it wasn't the western expo-
sure my husband decided he wanted so he could enjoy
the sunsets. We kept this property on our excruciatingly
thin "possibles" list.

Mona had a few more unimpressive places to show us
before she announced that in another week we'd have
seen everything on the market there was to see. That was
disheartening. We began trolling the Internet for properties Mona might not be showing us. We came across
one contemporary that sounded promising. It seemed to
have the square footage we desired, nice acreage, and
was definitely in our price range. We decided that when
Mona finished showing us all the properties, we'd inves-
tigate this particular one ourselves.

We began poring over information sheets of the
houses we'd seen, trying to pick the least worst. I suddenly had an insight, turned to my husband, and
announced that we were putting ourselves into a frame
of mind where we felt we had to choose one of the
houses we'd seen. But why should we have to settle for
less than what we wanted? "After all," I moaned, "I didn't
go through ten months of us living in separate states,
packing, selling our house, and moving, just to live in a
raised ranch." I envisioned a house and property so spec-
tacular that I'd have to pinch myself and ask rhetorically,
"Do I *really* live here?"

We discussed giving up the search for a year, and
waiting for the following spring. We were renting a
nice enough, very inexpensive apartment in a converted

Victorian-style house, and we could wait the market out. I also pulled out a design book and, combining designs I liked, began sketching the house of my dreams. If worst came to worst, we could always buy a chunk of land and build our dream home, but after having just spent ten years remodeling our New York home our- selves, neither of us had the desire to do it all over again. I halfheartedly told my husband I could summon the energy and fortitude if I had to. It was a daunting prospect that we didn't want to face, but would if it came to that. We had choices.

Our search for a home had begun in the southern portion of Coos County, and with each unsuccessful house hunt, Mona took us northward. In two weeks we'd have exhausted every available property all the way to the Canadian border. We were starting to run out of hope when Mona took us out one day and drove for a very long time. Being new to the area, I had no clue where we were, but my husband, having transferred ten months earlier, was mildly familiar with the next town we visited.

Mona pulled into the driveway of a building on Main Street, and we were met by another Realtor, who took us to several homes. The first was a Federal-style farmhouse that, while it had great mountain views, also had a large hole in the ground where an inground swimming pool had once been, and there wasn't a tree for miles. It was a white box sitting in the middle of nowhere. The inte- rior was lovely, with newly refinished hardwood floors, and the house went on our list of possibles. However, it didn't knock our socks off.

Next we visited a home with a new gambrel-roofed addition on ten acres. While it had sounded promising, the interior of the house was unfinished, and the gambrel addition was above the garage, making it impractical to hoist my husband's large and heavy machinery upstairs, not to mention bring in large sections of wood, or get a piece of finished furniture in or out. The ten acres was mostly swamp. Another disappointment.

We thought we'd reached rock bottom when we were shown a house on a road named Eagle's Nest that was purported to have views into Canada. We were all excited by the prospect and eagerly headed up the private dirt road. Once we stepped out of the car, we had to make a mad dash into the house as the black-fly population had just hatched and the bloodsuckers were all over us. I gazed out the living room windows, mesmerized by the number of hummingbirds on the lilacs, while my husband talked statistics with the owners. There were three bedrooms, two of which were unfinished, but if we had a mind to do it, there were stacks of sheetrock piled up in the rooms. The water for the house was from a gravity-fed well. That didn't put me off until the homeowner told us that his property, and all of the property surrounding it, was open to hunting, and that at the end of one hunting season he'd found the rotting carcass of a moose up the hill from the well. Mmmmm. Nothing like the bacteria from decaying flesh finding its way into your drinking water. The final turnoff was the drain the owner had built in the middle of the foundation floor so the blood and guts from dressing a moose would easily wash down and out. How thoughtful!

We bid the agent farewell, and thought we were done house hunting for the day, but Mona surprised us by meeting with a second Realtor. We began heading even farther north, past the town, past houses, past anything. We abruptly turned up a winding dirt road that seemed to go on forever. The climb was so steep that our ears popped. I noticed nothing along either side of the road except long stretches of forest, interrupted occasionally by a very nice house or two.

As we reached what I thought was the apex of the hill, we took yet another turn, this time up a single-lane dirt path that didn't even pass for a road, and then onto an even narrower path. Trees lined the way, obliterating everything from view except the huge mountain ahead. The driveway opened to a magnificent, rustic, contemporary home, and a mountain view to die for. Mona and the other agent went into the house while my husband and I remained in the car, speechless. As we looked at the printout Mona had just handed us, I pointed out to my husband that it was the house we'd seen on the Internet.

We spent the first ten minutes just walking around the untamed property atop the hill. The view was panoramic, with mountains in every direction. The only sound was the wind rustling through the trees, and the birds singing their joy. At that point, we almost didn't care how the house looked; we were sold on the location.

Stepping through the doorway, we were astounded. The entire house had soaring cathedral ceilings, the rooms were huge, the wall of windows viewed the mountains in every light, every change of season. With every turn it just got better and better. We knew this house was *it*. We excitedly made plans as we drove back to our apartment. I pulled out the dream-home sketch I'd drawn. It was remarkably, and eerily, similar to the house we'd just made an offer on.

Unlike New York closings, which tend to become acrimonious because the buyers, their attorney, and their broker, always seem to think the seller is deceitful, the New Hampshire closing was friendly. The first reason for this cordiality is that the area is minuscule, and not only do the real estate agents know each other well, chances are they are distant relatives. They also handle all of the contractual matters. An attorney is only brought into the picture to preside over the actual closing, and represents both sides. There are no extra fees or waiting for a deed. The attorney simply walks across the street to the courthouse to register the deed, get it stamped with the seal of approval, and it is in your hands minutes later.

The second reason for this stress-free atmosphere is that, in this part of the country, people assume you're as honest and up front about things as they are. In fact, our closing took only fifteen minutes, and there was so much amiable banter I thought we'd all be going to lunch afterward.

As I write this tale, the wind is rustling through the trees, the birds sing their songs of joy. I sit at the computer in front of the wall of windows of that house perched high atop the hill. Trees and mountains are all that are visible as far as the eye can see. The hawks fly past the window, and the night air is filled with the hoot of the barred owl. Occasionally, when the wind blows hard in a certain direction, there is a brief, faint whiff of "spring in the air."

2

When Realtors Are Helpful (or Not!)

Sanity Quiz

Jane, the Realtor you've signed with to sell your home, isn't getting the job done. The house has been on the market for over a year and you have yet to see an offer. Not only that, but for the last three months you haven't seen hide nor hair of a prospective buyer. But you do see Jane. She is down the block at the Ryans' property almost daily showcasing their home.

Do you
A. call Jane and immediately demand she get back to actively selling your house
B. stake out the Ryans' property and cause a big scene when Jane arrives with her next prospects
C. tell Jane you no longer feel she is the right one for the job
D. cancel your contract and find yourself another agent

No matter how you answered these questions, read on and discover how these contributors dealt with various Realtor blunders and still managed to jet the job done. And you thought it was just you!

Seven Steps to Surviving Realtors

Ray Zardetto

THE ONLY WAY to truly eliminate all of the stress and strain associated with buying a house is to decide *not* to buy one. Why put yourself through the modern-day equivalent of medieval thumbscrews?

You think there's a garden of green to be made by cashing in on the appreciation of your current house? Wait and see what the sandstorm of capital gains and other taxes does to your little oasis. (Hint: watch out for scorpions!)

You think you need a bigger house, more living space? If you decided to go that route, you will need to watch out for The Law of Inevitable Clutter—an immutable law of physics that states that any and all empty space in a house will inevitably be filled by an incalculable volume of semi-necessary furniture, unneeded knickknacks, stuff that will surely sell at next year's garage sale (but never does), and "there's-no-way-I-can-throw-these-out" mementos.

If you are still not dissuaded, and the urge to buy a home is beyond your ability to control, then I suggest you read the following Seven Survival Steps for Dealing with Realtors. It will help you preserve your sanity and assure your success. These tips have been hard won by yours truly after buying and selling six homes.

Tip #1: Understand the Professional Identity Crisis

People who recognize their strengths usually put them to work in an appropriate industry. For instance, if you find you have a talent for drawing, you become an animator or graphic artist. If you have an excellent command of the language, you can become a writer. If you have a knack for advanced math and spatial relationships, then an engineering career is probably in your future. You won't find many people who say, "Gee whiz, I understand biology and anatomy very well and I know a lot about medicine, but instead of being a doctor, I think I would rather drive around with one of those Century 21 signs pasted to the door of my car."

As far as I can tell, full-time Realtors are people who have not yet identified their own talents. I believe that to be the case because I cannot think of any particular talent or aptitude that would compel someone to cry out, "I must put this talent to work selling houses!"

This hint may or may not help you buy a house. I'm just suggesting that Realtors are sensitive about this stuff—so don't make fun of them.

Tip #2: Realize that Intelligence Is Preferred but Not Required

There is a great range of smarts in the real estate business—I think it is because the process of qualifying to become a Realtor is available to most everyone. Almost all the Realtors I have met were nice people. Some were sharp as tacks. Others, to be honest, were among the dullest knives in the drawer. That tells me that while intelligence in a Realtor is preferred, it is not a requirement. That should be comforting news to Paris Hilton, should she ever contemplate a career change—from whatever her career is right now.

Again, I'm not sure how helpful this tip will be, but I grab any opportunity I can to make fun of Ms. Hilton.

Tip #3: Watch the Language!

In the early stages of working with a Realtor, they will see you as a client and treat you as such. But if the sales process drags on, they may begin to see you as a two-legged impediment to their sales commission. Ever

anxious to earn that commission, they might, on occasion, overenthusiastically describe some of the properties
they are trying to sell.

Not to say that Realtors would lie, but some of their
statements could be, shall we say, veracity-challenged. To
Realtors, a house with a major thoroughfare running
through the backyard is "convenient to local highways
and transportation"; a house where the heat and hot
water do not work has "old world charm"; any structure
with a roof and four walls is described as "in move-in
condition." Heck, they'd call the Unabomber's shack a
"unique fixer-upper opportunity."

Tip #4: Know that What You See May Not Be What You Get

Don't evaluate a house by the lousy photos you see in
the newspaper ads and brochures. Either Realtors
don't understand the power of the visual or they all use
Mr. Magoo as their photographer. I can't count how
many photos I've see in which an overgrown bush or
tree limb hides half the front of the house, or the
photo of the house is taken at a bad angle, or the photo
is so poorly lit that it is actually in black and white—
without the white. This is not to say that most houses
will be better in the flesh. Just as often, a photo can be
deceiving in the other direction. I mean, ever heard of
Photoshop? The moral of the story: See for yourself.

Tip #5: Avoid the 10 Percent Phenomenon

Tell your Realtor the maximum amount of money you want to spend when you start the process of buying a house—then watch how every house you are shown, as if by magic, is "just a little bit more than your price range." If you tell them your limit is $200,000, be prepared to see houses in the range of $220,000 to $225,000. If you point out the discrepancy in the cost, expect the Realtor to shake it off with a smile and point out that the extra money will mean "only a few extra mortgage payments . . . no big deal." But, if you suggest they cut the price of the house and eliminate those extra mortgage payments, you will see how suddenly important that 10 percent is to the buyer.

Tip #6: Inspect the Inspectors

Home inspectors are supposed to complete a thorough check of the house and, with a keen and expert eye, point out flaws or structural defects the prospective owner should know before closing the deal. My favorite part of dealing with home inspectors is the contract and the waiver clause you sign before they perform their service. In essence, it states that they will not be liable should they not find some defect or problem that later turns out to be a significant problem for you.

Huh?

That's like the coach of a sports team asking ownership to sign a waiver that he's not to blame for the team
losing because he didn't watch the whole game, or a
lawyer asking for a waiver in case he does not know all
the applicable laws. Personally, I think you would do just
as well with a big *How to Do Everything Around Your House*
book from Home Depot.

Tip #7: Strengthen Your Hand and Close Your Eyes

And speaking of lawyers . . . before you get to the closing, make sure you spend a week or two doing exercises
to strengthen your writing hand. You will need it to sign
your name about 500 times on the stacks of documents
waiting for you there. I have no idea what these piles of
paperwork are, but I think the sheer volume of sheets is
a lawyer's way of demonstrating all the work he or she
has done. Don't bother reading any of it—just sign
where they tell you to sign. Truth is, if you were to really
take a look at all these documents, all you would see is
the same line typed over and over and over: "All work
and no play makes Jack a dull boy" . . . just like that repeated line in the infamous novel Jack Nicholson's
character is writing in *The Shining*. And you know what
happened to *that* piece of property!

Keep these seven tips in mind, and no matter how difficult, tedious, or frustrating the home-buying process

becomes, remember that when it's completed, you will own your part of the American Dream! You will have graduated from home buyer to homeowner—and you will no longer have to worry about dealing with Realtors.

Instead, you can start worrying about replacing the antiquated heating system in your new house, caulking the bathroom fixtures, insulating the windows and doors, cleaning the carpets and floors, fixing the unhinged doors, and trimming back the overgrowing weeds around the porch.

Ah! The joys of homeownership!

Inching Our Way to Buying a House

Brian J. P. Craig

"THAT DOES IT, we're buying a house!"

I hoped my wife was venting, but doubted that was the case. We'd been married for eighteen months. I had just gotten home, and Barbara, an accountant, had spent the evening doing our taxes. I found her in tears, frustrated and angry. We owed the government $3,000, and Barbara was determined to get us a deduction before next year.

A friend told me, "Buying a house for a tax deduction is like taking an airplane flight for the peanuts," but Barbara and I had already planned to buy a house at some point. I wanted to wait another year; we were still paying off the wedding and we'd just renewed the lease on our apartment.

I knew I was going to be a homeowner sooner than I'd planned when Barbara started calling mortgage places the next day, looking for preapproval. The first place took her name and offered us a substantial loan of several hundred thousand dollars. The second place was more thorough; they asked how much we made before approving us for almost as much as the first one.

"Geez, stop calling places," I joked. "Each one thinks we're worth less than the one before!"

We started looking online for houses costing in the range of our preapproved mortgage. I also started researching towns. Honestly, I was trying to slow the process; I was worried about how fast this was happening! After a couple of weeks researching and visiting open houses, an interesting but futile exercise, Barbara was getting antsy and I was tired of stalling. Besides, I started to like the idea of owning a house. We decided to find a Realtor.

Finding a good real estate agent can be tricky. Or, you can rely on dumb luck. We saw two places online that interested us; both were represented by the same agent. I called the Realtor, Judy, and she had us come to her office that Saturday.

Judy was great. I brought the list of towns we were considering and printouts of places we'd seen online.

She skimmed the list, telling us where we could expect to find a place, and which towns were outside our price range. She flipped through the listings, tossing aside ones that were in bad areas. Then she sent us out with her husband, Joe. We looked at a couple of places and arranged to go out again with Joe the following Saturday.

During the week, I e-mailed Judy our thoughts about the houses we'd seen. When we returned to her office, Judy went over the list with us, to be sure that we weren't expecting too much. After a gentle but necessary reality check, she had us look at listings that she thought we'd be interested in. These seemed closer to what we had in mind, and we hit the road with Joe again.

Meanwhile, Barbara was still looking for a mortgage company she liked. She'd seen an ad and signed up for a free seminar for first-time home buyers. Everyone who attended would get preapproved without a filing fee. It sounded like a gimmick to me, but finances were Barbara's department; if she wanted to go, we'd go.

The seminar the following week was scheduled to start at 7:30 P.M. When the woman who ran the seminars let us in, she proved to be charming, chatty, and totally professional. Instead of inventing a number, she asked what we made, what we owed, what we currently paid in rent, and how much we felt comfortable paying monthly. Using that info, she worked backwards and said that we should look at houses about $25,000 less than we'd considered earlier; she could get us approval on that easily. Barbara and I were comfortable with her and her tactics, as well as the price recommendation. We changed our target price accordingly.

On Saturday, when I let Judy know about the change in our price tag, she sent an assistant to run a list of properties in our new price range. Then she looked at me seriously. "Listen," Judy said, "helping you guys find a house is my job, and I love it. You're not being a burden when you call me. If there's something you need to tell me, then I need to hear it." We promised to stay in contact, and left with Joe again.

Through Joe, we found two houses that interested us: a hundred-year-old farmhouse that had been in the same family for three generations, and a modern bi-level near Barbara's job. I'd seen the second house online and asked Judy about it, but when she looked it was gone. Two weeks later, it appeared in the system again. We liked both and asked Barbara's dad, a general contractor, if he'd give us his opinion. I was leaning toward the farmhouse; I liked the roominess of it. But I could tell that my father-in-law wasn't impressed. He seemed happier with the bi-level. We asked what he thought.

"They're both nice," he said, "but I think you're better off with the second one. There doesn't seem to be anything wrong with the first one now, but it's a hundred years old. Stuff is going to start to go, and you really won't have the money to do major repairs right away, will you?" He also pointed out that the farmhouse was in a town with one road in and out; rush hour would be a problem.

We bid on the bi-level. Two days later, Joe called with bad news. "That house had originally been under contract, but it looked like the deal was going to fall through, so they listed it again. Now, it looks like the original deal is back on. I'm going to pressure their Realtor to at least hear your bid, but I want to be in the best position I can. What is the absolute highest you'll go for that house?"

We told him, but he called back two days later to say that they didn't even hear our bid; they felt that they "owed" it to the original bidders. Barbara was disappointed. However, as much as I liked the house, I was well aware of its shortcomings. I was okay with the way things played out. Besides, I was still concerned about the yearlong lease on our apartment.

Our experience with the farmhouse narrowed our search. We eliminated towns that would make our commutes harder. We especially liked two lake communities. A few weeks after the bi-level fell through, we drove by a house in one of the lake communities that appealed to us. Although the house was in the system, Joe explained that nobody could show it until the following Sunday. Barbara had a good feeling about it, so we told Joe that we wanted to see it.

The following Sunday, we met Joe and went to the house. We were the first ones to see the place, and we liked it . . . a lot. We walked out—Barbara bouncing up and down with a big grin on her face—and told Joe that we'd pay the asking price. It was at the high end of our range, but we were sure.

On Monday Joe called us, again with bad news. The homeowner had received three other bids, all higher than ours. He asked if we wanted to go any higher. I said we'd go up another ten thousand.

"That's it," I told him. "I'm not getting into a bidding war for any house, and I really think that's what they wanted to happen."

When we didn't get the house, Barbara was devastated. She said she was starting to think we'd never find a house. I told her not to worry, but the search had started to lose its novelty. A good part of every weekend was spent house hunting. Joe was fun to be with, but I started to feel guilty taking up so much of his time.

A few weeks later, Joe and Judy went to Florida, and we went out with an associate, Dan, whom Joe was training. Dan took us to a pretty little lake community and showed us a house that we fell in love with: a small, hilltop bungalow near the lake, the pool, and the tennis and basketball courts. The backyard was huge, and the screened porch seemed ideal for reading on summer evenings. Moreover, the family living there didn't want to close until the end of the summer, giving our apartment complex three more months to rent our place! It seemed perfect.

They were asking quite a bit more than our price. We asked Dan if he thought they'd take what we could offer. Dan called Joe and Judy, who said, "Hey, if that's what you want to offer, go ahead. You're in the ballpark, and the worst they can do is say no. Hopefully, it'll open up negotiations."

Judy was right. We split the difference and bought the house.

Our mortgage broker arranged the extra financing. Joe came to the inspection, which went well, and the walk-through, which somehow the homeowner didn't know about. It was a slightly embarrassing situation, but after everything was cleared up, we all laughed.

Then, Joe called right before the final papers were signed. The earlier deal for the house in the other lake community had fallen through; the owner wondered if we were still interested. But we were so happy with our little bungalow that we said no.

So we got our house, and settled in to a nice quiet life . . . until eighteen months later, when I came home from work and my wife said, "I think we can expand the house now. We should have enough equity to build out the back and add on a second floor!"

God, I love her.

SURVIVAL HINTS

1. Know what you want and be specific about it. If you're just looking for "a house," you could wind up settling.

2. Enjoy the process of buying a home because it could take a while. If you view it as an adventure, you can have fun. If you view it as a chore, you can lose your mind.

3. Professionalism counts. If someone quotes facts and figures with little (or nothing) to back them up, they're probably not someone you should deal with.

4. Work with people you like, because you'll be spending a lot of time with them. There are all kinds of professionals; some are super serious, some are clowns. You may as well have fun while you're looking.

5. Don't get discouraged. No house is perfect. If you lose a place you love, you'll probably wind up getting one that you love even more.

Be Careful What You Wish For

Carole A. Daley

IF ONLY SOMEONE had protected us from ourselves.

The birth of our daughter marked the onset of re-ordered thinking. No more rentals for us; it was time to become grown-ups with a mortgage and the promise of building equity. Spending money on dinners, movies, plays, and vacations was out. Mortgage payments and leftovers were in. Our two-bedroom apartment now seemed frivolous, even though it was only a ten-minute commute to work by car or city bus. Didn't responsible parents provide a home with a yard for their children?

With little down payment, but two incomes and a fist-ful of credit cards, we began our search. Real estate prices were breathtaking. When we found ourselves wondering if a walk-in closet would be sufficient as a bedroom for our daughter, we gave up on buying a home in San Francisco. Sacrificing the excitement and beauty of San Francisco for wide-open spaces, better schools, and a backyard for our progeny was the key to happiness, wasn't it?

We decided it was time to enlist the aid of a Realtor and we found Richard, or maybe he found us. I suspect we met him at one of the open houses we diligently took in every weekend. Richard never seemed to tire of showing us real estate in our price range. The only problem was we didn't like anything we could afford. What we could afford were mostly worn-out rentals that owners had decided to cash in on. My enthusiasm slipped away on the day Richard showed us one of these special properties and I had to gingerly climb over a sleeping figure passed out on the floor. "It just needs some TLC," Richard cooed.

Our search for suburban nirvana finally ended in a subdivision with the charming name of Peacock Gap. Big homes with big yards were situated next to fifteen miles of hiking trails threading through 1,600 acres along the shores of San Francisco Bay. Richard enticed us with boasts of wildlife watching, hiking, swimming, boating, windsurfing, and more than 200 fog-free days per year. Best of all, it was a mere twenty-three miles from San Francisco.

A few weeks after we closed on our new home, Richard presented us with a framed pen-and-ink drawing of the house. My husband Jim and I started at it in disbelief. The artist had captured what we had yet to process in our parental earnestness. The house was coyote ugly. A tiny lone sapling stood off to one side of the blockish, gray house. The wide driveway had no elegant curve; it was just an expanse of concrete. The overall impression was of a big, fat toad sitting on a rock in the hot sun.

I glanced into Richard's face, expecting to see an impish grin, some sign of a joke, but all I saw was sincerity as he held up the bland picture in its beige frame. But we were still brimming with determination to make this work. Thinking it would ease us into a suburban frame of mind, we bought an SUV with our dwindling supply of credit and taught the au pair how to drive.

The commute was unavoidable and tough—from door to door it was ninety minutes by bus, or two hours by ferry, or an eternity by car. In a desperate attempt to beat the morning commuter traffic, we joined a health club in the Financial District, just blocks from our offices. Waking from a sound sleep in the predawn hours, we would pull on workout attire, grab our work clothes and toiletries, and head for the highway, leaving the au pair and our child still sleeping.

On top of the long commute we were now becoming sleep-deprived since our daughter had become restless almost every night. One deafeningly quiet Sunday afternoon, Jim, being exhausted and frustrated by no sleep, finally snapped. "I'm leaving, with you or without you!" he roared. Without stopping to take a breath, he continued, "and every time I take Caitlin to the park, the other parents talk to me."

"That's called being neighborly," I told him dryly.

Jim continued his tirade. "We've lived here for seven months and I am tired of getting up at five to drive into San Francisco to work out and shower in a gym just to avoid traffic. Coming home takes over an hour—and it's less than thirty miles away! You don't mind because you aren't doing the driving, you're sleeping! I'm sick of leaving home in the dark and returning in the dark. I don't know why I hate this place so much; I've never even seen it in daylight!"

I didn't bother to point out that his last point was an exaggeration. We had all seen the house in daylight. The carpet was brown, black, and gray. It definitely hid the dirt. The house lacked air-conditioning (Richard had assured us it wasn't necessary). He may have been right, but huge curtainless windows ringed the top of the two-story living room walls and turned the house into an oven. Except for the commute, these problems could have been solved if we hadn't spent every penny we had, and a lot of pennies that we didn't have.

The au pair was the next to fold. She threatened to leave if we didn't reduce her hours to a more reasonable forty hours a week. As for me, until our latest foray into the outback, I had spent my life escaping from and then avoiding the suburbs. After my initial break from suburban hell, I lived in London, Los Angeles, Chicago, and San Francisco, and loved every crowded, polluted moment. My husband wasn't going to get any argument from me about bailing out.

So I called Richard to talk about selling our gray whale, and Jim and I began hunting for shelter in San Francisco. When we met with Richard to sign the listing agreement, I couldn't help but think of the Walrus from *Through the Looking Glass,* by Lewis Carroll. "It seems a shame," the Walrus said, "to play them such a trick, after we've brought them out so far, and made them trot so quick!"

SURVIVAL HINTS

1. No Realtor can be all things to all people. Decide where your Realtor's strengths lie and then take special care where they are weak.

2. Realtors are only human (imagine that!). There are only so many geographic areas they can intimately acquaint themselves with. Most Realtors are happy to venture outside of their comfort zones—after all, no sales, no commission. Realtors have lots of information at their fingertips, but in less familiar territory, they'll need lots of input from you.

3. Don't skip any of the inspections. Follow the inspectors around to see what problems there are, and to get to know the house. You'll find out where the heater is, how long the roof is going to last, and if there any special maintenance needs.

4. Be brutally honest with yourself and your loved ones about what you need in a living environment.

Backing into a Beach House

Arline Simpson

REALTORS CAN MAKE all the difference when you're
buying a house, even if you're not really looking for one.
Let me explain: My husband and I had always taken vacations with our children during the Christmas holidays,
usually going to the Catskills for the week between
Christmas and New Year's. But that year, 1982, I wanted
an extra winter weekend getaway of a different sort,
minus the kids, and despite my husband's preference for
yet another trip to the Catskills. I objected, not because
I didn't like the Catskills, but because it just wasn't the
kind of vacation I needed.

Being a mom with three small kids and having
gained a considerable amount of weight, I thought a
spa would be healthier for me and more enjoyable, too.

The last thing I needed was the hotel plan of the Catskills, which included three huge meals a day and offered very limited physical activities for those who don't ski, ice-skate, ride horses, or enjoy any of the other winter sports that were abundant there. By contrast, we'd spent several lovely weekends in the Hamptons, on Long Island in New York. The Hamptons then were not the fancy, upscale place of today. And Montauk, a small fishing village at the very end of Long Island, was the least pretentious of all.

During the winter months, many Montauk residents used to escape to Florida or the Bahamas. Those who remained were mostly fisherman and small retail shopkeepers, mostly drugstores, a few restaurants, Laundromats, real estate offices, gas stations, and several other service businesses. Gurney's Inn was a major attraction there year-round. A world-renowned international spa, Gurney's offers guests a variety of spa and salon services including myriad massage and skin-care options, diets, exercise programs, steam, sauna and whirlpool treatments, and an indoor Olympic-size saltwater pool. There was also entertainment and dancing after dinner, and the restaurant and service were superb. It offered exactly what I felt I needed at that time.

But my husband insisted that it was folly to go to the beach in the winter. He had his heart set on the Catskills. And I disagreed. Walks along the beach and on the dunes were both relaxing and invigorating, even in the winter. Announcing that I needed a low-calorie, healthy vacation and would go without him if necessary, I insisted we head for Montauk. Reluctantly, he gave in.

We left on a Friday afternoon. The weather was cold and gray, and the drive took two and a half hours. My husband would have been happier driving north to the Catskills instead of east, but he was resigned to going to Montauk by now. Eventually we arrived and checked in at the spa. The next day after my massage, facial, and an exercise class, we drove into town.

Looking to do a little sightseeing and to pass the time, we wandered into a Realtor's office and asked if they would show us some houses. There we met a Realtor, Bridgette, a delightful woman who agreed to take us around and show us what was available. Did we actually plan to buy? No. But it was a pleasant way to spend the day.

The first house she showed us was definitely a handyman special. It was owned by a divorced gentleman who was planning to remarry and relocate. His three children lived with him, and they also had several animals, all of which had left their signatures on the carpeting, walls, floors, etc. The owner's fiancée had made new curtains for the windows and tried her best to pretty up the place, but it needed a lot more than curtains. The property itself, however, was fabulous. It featured a large front yard and an even larger wooded backyard that was full of potential. We looked, chatted, and then moved on to the other houses.

Bridgette showed us five more places. We thanked her profusely, told her we would be in touch and then we returned to Gurney's in time for dinner. Naturally, our conversation turned to the properties we saw. I was very enthusiastic about the first house; I saw *so* much potential. All it needed was a good paint job, some new carpeting, and eventually replacements of both the front and back porches. My husband, however, was not convinced. I reminded him that the kids were growing up, and that soon they wouldn't want to go to camp. The house had a great location, being a mile or so from the beach or the fishing boats, and, best of all, it was close to a state park with a swimming pool right near the street. And the price was right. My husband argued that he was not handy; the house might cost a fortune to fix up. But I reminded him how much he hated to travel, especially by plane, and this would be just a car ride, with no planes or trains or luggage.

Mind you, this was all still a completely hypothetical conversation. It hadn't even reached the more serious "discussion" stage yet. But talking about it in the abstract got us both thinking, even though we really weren't actually looking to buy anything—especially not a fixer-upper.

The next day, we spoke not a word about it on the ride home. But I was very excited about the idea of buying the Montauk house, and a call to Bridgette the Realtor reassured me that the house was not likely to sell quickly in the dead of winter. As for my husband, I assumed he'd dismissed the whole thing, and decided to wait a bit to press my case.

Then, not more than a week had passed when my husband called me at my office.

"You know my client, Max?" he asked.

"Yes," I replied. "What about him?"

"He wants to lend somebody money at a decent interest rate and I told him to lend it to me!"

"Why?" I asked.

What he said next nearly floored me.

"Because he can give us a mortgage on our house, and then we can buy the house on Montauk."

"Which one?" I asked.

"The fixer-upper, of course!" was his reply.

Needless to say I was surprised and thrilled. After all his reluctance to even visit Montauk in the winter, now he'd found a way to buy the house I loved!

When we got home from our respective businesses that evening, we talked excitedly about how crazy it was that we hadn't even been looking to buy anything, especially in the Hamptons. Apparently he'd fallen in love with the house and the town too, but just wasn't ready to admit it right away. I didn't realize that despite my husband's objections, he'd been slowly getting used to the idea of buying that house, and he kept envisioning our kids and all their friends enjoying the area, going to the beach, and enjoying the summers in the peaceful community that would bring them so much fun. That house and all its possibilities—and the pleasant time we'd spent looking at the quiet, pretty neighborhoods, and getting to know Montauk a bit, had actually haunted us both.

When all was said and done, we both felt good about the decision to go for it. I couldn't wait to tell our kids, and I agreed to my husband's plan to borrow the money from the client. And no more fattening trips to the Catskills—at least for a while.

Meanwhile, Bridgette had called to encourage us to make an offer, and was very confident that the house was a great buy. We worked closely with her, and made an offer, which to our delight was accepted immediately. Bridgette arranged all the paperwork for the closing, helping us every step of the way. If it hadn't been for her making it all so seamless for us, things might have ultimately fallen through, because my husband and I both have our own very demanding businesses and wouldn't have been able to deal with too many outside hassles or complications. But Bridgette made the whole process flow as smoothly as could be and we were all delighted with the end result.

We bought the house in June, and cleaning it up was a major project. When we showed the Montauk house to my in-laws, they turned pale and wondered if we had gone crazy. But soon the kids were playing in the back-yard. Bridgette, who was becoming a friend, came to visit with her husband, and he suggested my husband start a garden. Now, my beloved had never planted so much as a window box, let alone a whole garden, and prior to purchasing our home in New Jersey, we had both grown up in apartments in New York City. While I had always wanted a house, my husband didn't even want a flowerpot! Yet somehow there we were—with not one house, but two! And to all our family's amazement, each summer my unhandy husband planted a huge and bountiful garden from which we fed all our neighbors there and in New Jersey with fresh vegetables, while our son, who had become an expert fisherman, supplied fresh fish to everyone we knew.

We've now owned our house in Montauk for twenty-five years. With some hard work, a little money, and a lot of dedication, we made a weekend life there and our extended family enjoys it year-round, especially the grandchildren.

Who would have thought that our weekend at Gurney's and a casual day of recreational house hunting with Bridgette would lead to a lifetime of friendship and relaxing year-round weekends for all of us? We're all very glad we skipped that fattening trip to the Catskills!

3

When You're Buying a Newly Built House

Sanity Quiz

You've done everything you can to make the process of building your home as problem free as possible. However, with each step you take, you hit another hurdle, some of gigantic proportion, some minor. Now your contractors just aren't getting the work done on schedule. Every time you visit the site they seem to be taking another break.

Do you
A. read them the riot act
B. fire them and hire others
C. stay on site to put the pressure on
D. offer to help them in any way you can

No matter which answer you chose, you'll benefit from reading how our contributors coped. And you think you have problems?

Closing, Then Camping

Tina Martinez

MY HUSBAND, GEORGE, and I found our dream home—3,000 square feet, two stories, and a full base-ment in the making. The fixtures were top of the line, every countertop, including the kitchen and three and a half baths, was granite, and gleaming hardwood floors were being installed on all three levels in our brand new house! Even more exciting than the numer-ous upgrades, we were thrilled to find a buyer for our current home in only two weeks. This move seemed to be in the cards and in the stars, because everything was coming together swiftly and easily.

The only tricky part was the closing date proposed for our buyers—they wanted to close in a month—just a day or two short of our new house's completion date.

The buyers were moving from a long distance and both needed to be settled in to start their new jobs. After talking to our builder, we were confident that everything would work out fine. The buyers' closing date would perfectly correspond to the closing date of our new home.

With both their and our moving vans packed, we headed to the title company to close on both houses. The buyers' closing went smoothly, no surprises, and we shook their hands and wished them luck with the house we'd enjoyed for five years. Then, immediately after our buyers walked out through the big mahogany doors, the seller/developer walked in with terrible news—the house would not be finished today! Worse, we had given our buyers immediate occupancy. Looking out the window I could see the buyers stepping into their U-Haul and driving away to unload their stuff into our just-sold house. There was no turning back. Were we going to be homeless?

Fortunately, the developer explained that the city's code inspector had provided a certificate of occupancy, which meant that our new house would be legally habitable. Then our savvy real estate lawyer negotiated a quick deal, including complex mumbo jumbo such as escrowing the work to be completed. So at least we could close the deal on our new house. But we had to agree to endure the continuing work in the house, which mostly consisted of putting finish on the hardwood floors. All we would have to do is deal with contractors who would need daily access to the house for a couple of weeks. We agreed—after all, this really was no big deal.

Boy, were we wrong!

Our movers pulled up their van at our new house shortly after our closing. Fortunately, by doubling the size of our living space, we had twice the space to hold the van's contents. The movers placed everything carefully on the main floor's hardwood, which was covered by padding, then left. Then the workers arrived to begin staining the basement floors, so we decided to get to work—but what work? We couldn't unpack—two floors of hardwood needed to be stained and sealed. And how and where would we move our stuff when it was time to work on the main floor? The top floor? Our backs wouldn't be able to stand this constant rearranging on one floor, much less up and down stairs. And where were we going to sleep? At least one floor would be wet, and the fumes would be unbearable.

Instead of throwing a fit or getting upset, I came up with a few suggestions: Should we ask to stay a couple of weeks with friends? No, with short notice this would be a real imposition. Maybe we could split the difference and take two out-of-town trips to see our parents? Uh, no, that's not a very appealing option. Sleep in a hotel? That's too much money, and, in hindsight, a hotel stay should have been negotiated with the developer. Sleep in the garage—no, that's where we'd have to store our belongings until the floors were finished.

"Hey!" George said, "let's go camping!" After all, it was the hottest part of summer, we camped often, owned a big tent, and there was a big backyard freshly covered with sod on which we could pitch it. So we called the movers back to move our load into the garage while we pitched our unexpected temporary home.

In no time, we had set up our tent, established a functional campground kitchen with our gas grill, and a billowy bed with our bed's mattress and comforter! We plugged in our fridge in the garage and filled it with campy foods—hot dogs and chickens for grilling, steaks and hamburgers with potatoes and buns. Soda, beer, chips and dips, and even ingredients for s'mores! Wine and a boom box made us think we were on vacation. It was a ball! Each night we'd come home from work, park in the garage, grab a lawn chair, fire up the grill, and pop a bottle of chardonnay. We even invited our new neighbors to join in—what an icebreaker!

Our floors were finally finished and ready to walk on, the movers resumed their work, and we took down the tent. Still, living in that tent was so much fun that we sometimes think about camping out again in the backyard. But we don't. After all, our neighbors might think we're really loony!

SURVIVAL HINTS

1. Try to find fun things to do that will bring you closer to your loved ones instead of getting pissy about the hassles of moving.
2. With the proper attitude, you can make lemonade out of lemons.

Trust Your Decisions

P. J. Dempsey

MY HUSBAND AND I live in a tiny New York City apartment and we needed a quiet place to get away on the weekends. We were both raised in houses so our priority was not to buy a larger apartment in the city but to own a home with a front and backyard—our little slice of heaven.

Our foray into homeownership was done pretty much the way we do everything—we sort of head off in a direction and learn as we go, hoping things come together. Surprisingly, things always work out for the best, eventually, if we go with the flow and take the bad with the good. The trick is to try not to take too much control when things go wrong, to view the process as a whole.

In this case, however, we didn't even know which state we wanted to live in on weekends. I had visions of living in a lovingly restored older home, but my husband was dreaming of building a new home because he had never lived in a new one.

So to get the ball rolling, he appeared one day with a copy of a popular New York newspaper that had a double-page advertisement from a builder proclaiming that the Poconos was the perfect place for country living and was also convenient to New York City. The ad said that all we had to do was go and look for ourselves—and we'd even be reimbursed our traveling expenses.

We called the toll-free number and set up an appointment for the following Saturday morning. An hour later, we were whisked around the Pocono Mountains where we viewed potential home sites. True to our nature, we found the perfect setting that day for our home (actually two adjoining lots). We fell in love with the land because we loved the ferns covering the property. (Only later did we learn that ferns need wetlands to grow this beautifully.) We signed on the dotted line, and a few weeks later started designing our house, or rather personalizing the model home. There was no turning back.

One-stop shopping is what the builder offered, but we wanted more. We wanted a screened porch, a full basement with rough plumbing for a future powder room, a long driveway, ceramic tile in the master bathroom and kitchen (not the linoleum they offered), a Jacuzzi in the master bathroom, and enough windows for cross-ventilation in every room so that we could enjoy the natural air-conditioning of the mountain air. Yes, they said, it could all be done—which led my husband to proclaim loudly, and for many years to come, that building a house was like ordering a pizza—you could add anything you wanted, but it would cost you.

Now, going to a builder/developer is not like going to an architect to build your dream house. Builders offer certain options and some of the options may even be upgraded (like quality of flooring) for a price. If you want something they do not offer (like the Jacuzzi), you buy it, have it delivered to the site, and hope they know how install it correctly. This wasn't always the case with our builder. This particular option is like gambling: sometimes you lose and, very rarely, you win—and if you're really lucky, you'll come out even.

Another thing to remember is that builder/developers are often putting up a number of houses at the same time, which explained the double-wide interior doors that showed up in our house and stayed for a number of weeks until someone figured out that they were the missing special order for a wheelchair-accessible house being built a number of miles away in a different development.

What I also didn't realize was that my husband had no intention of ever talking to a builder or a lawyer without a go-between—*me!* This is why many couples become uncoupled during the home-building process—one of them just can't cope. I was willing to take on the task because I do like things done my way, but as it turned out my husband didn't want to take part in anything. He'd sign the checks because he wanted to move into a perfect new home, but he didn't want any of the aggravation.

The problem with his desire to sign checks and deal directly with no one, however, was that at the time we were dealing with this (twenty years ago now), most of the women in that particular nonurban setting were wives or secretaries. This meant that these construction types could not relate to, nor were they about to take orders from, the five-foot-two-inch wife, even if she had a management job at a publishing company! This unfortunate fact is what challenged my husband's exalted position as Lord of the Manor who blissfully watched as the minions magically got things done. Reluctantly, he became the go-between, but I still called the shots. It worked, more or less, until the construction types felt that they could pull the wool over the city slickers' eyes. Case in point, the unplanned, indoor, basement swimming pool. Building a house with a fully underground basement in the wetlands is not ideal. An architect would have pointed this out or revised the plans accordingly; a developer will do or try to do whatever you will pay for.

It all turned out fine, eventually, but pumping the water out of the basement and pouring the concrete was the last thing to be done in that house before we moved in. Oh, yes, and there was also the lawyer we needed to hire to make sure the water did get pumped out. Oh, and let's not forget the purchase of that marvelous invention, the sump pump (another term added to our home-building vocabulary) to keep it pumped out. In the end we had the driest basement on the street.

We lived happily on weekends in that house for almost eight years in the quiet splendor of the mountains among the deer, bears, raccoons, turtles, and possum. What happened next was that the rest of civilization found us. Houses were built all around our sanctuary, relegating the very large bay window in the bathroom, which allowed us to bathe in our "Jacuzzi with the view," to peep-show status!

We reasoned that this was our starter weekend house, and that now it was time to put the house on the market and move on. It stayed on the market for two and a half years. Granted, from the outside it looked like a lot of other houses built at that time in the Poconos, even though it was so much more than that on the inside. Ultimately, none of it mattered.

We finally dropped the price to almost half of what we'd paid to build it, rationalizing that it was still less than if we'd rented a place. Having only a fifteen-year mortgage also helped, so we knew we'd still be walking away with enough to make a down payment on another house—one we would buy already built!

Real estate brokers loved our house but couldn't sell it. They hinted that the location was not working to our advantage. The fact that our new next-door neighbors built close to the edge of their lot, almost on our driveway, and cut down every single tree on their property in order to have a lawn (In the mountains? Don't get me started!) didn't help.

Just when we thought we'd never sell the place, one snowy January day there was a knock on the door. A real estate agent (not ours) happened to be driving past our house. It seems that she got lost while looking for another house to show her clients. Frustrated at not being able to find that house, she took advantage of our For Sale sign to save face with the family she was inadvertently taking on a tour of the Pocono Mountains.

As luck would have it, our selling price was in their price range, and we sold our house that day. Not only that, but it seems that we'd both always dreamed of living in a log house, but thought it too much to hope for. The timing was perfect (and so was the price), but the path to it wasn't a straight one. We now live in our total dream house made of logs—and this time we found it in only one day!

SURVIVAL HINTS

1. When considering building, know what you're in for in terms of time and money.
2. Don't build the most expensive house in the neighborhood, otherwise you'll have trouble recouping your expenses when you sell.
3. Be sure to check zoning laws to avoid being crowded in later by new neighbors who may build too close to your lot for comfort!
4. Keep the lines of communication open and share the stress. Building a house exacerbates or creates problems in all relationships.

A Rock in a Hard Place

Pam Brodowsky

PLANNING OUR HOUSE was not a problem. We knew exactly what we wanted, easily found what we thought were the right contactors, breezed through the loan process at the local bank, and were on our way. The problems for us didn't start until the actual work had begun.

We had some acreage in a rather beautiful secluded spot on top of a mountain with a gorgeous panoramic view. But the only thing a mountain sits upon is a rock— and rock it was from about two inches down to eternity.

Since our home builder was a "do-it-all" contractor we had also contracted him to dig the foundation, figuring hiring one person to do more than one thing was easier. We thoroughly warned him of the rock situation and he assured us over and over again that he would have no problem taking care of it. But even with our in-depth description I still had the distinct feeling he wasn't seeing the entire picture. Noticing that I was a bit wary of his confidence, he again assured us he would take care of it. The charge for the foundation: $12,000, which was the bid he had given us, and which we submitted to the bank for inclusion in the loan. As far as we were concerned it was a done deal.

Day one on the job site: My in-laws lived next door to the property so the goings-on of the contractors were easily monitored. About two hours into day one of the foundation digging I got a call at work saying all the contactors had left the site. I immediately called the builder and questioned the whereabouts of the workers.

"Well," he said, "we hit a rock."

"Yes, I told you that you'd hit rock," I responded.

"It's right in the middle of your house," he said.

"Yes. And?" I asked.

"We can't do anything else," he said.

"You've only been there for two hours and that includes the unloading and reloading of your heavy equipment. I hardly call that an effort," I said.

"Well, I'm sorry. The guys are leaving to work on another job."

I immediately called the bank and had them stop payment on the upfront money for the foundation. I then placed a call to a friend who lived near the property—a contractor himself—and asked him to take a look to see if he would be able to dig the foundation. He was a bit more daring than the original contractor, and said he'd give it a try. He dug out the entire foundation except for the large rock that was protruding up through the middle of where our home was supposed to be; it just wouldn't move. He explained that this last bit of rock was not a rock in the traditional sense but rather the tip of the ledge, a ledge that encompassed the whole span of mountain on which we were about to build.

"You're gonna have to blast," he told me.

"Blast! Blast!" I said, knowing there was no spare cash for it in our loan. "How much is that going to cost me?" He directed me to a guy he knew who would give us a good price.

I left work to meet with the blaster and once he had taken a look at the site he quoted us $3,850.00 to blast the remaining rock/ledge to create the hole for the foundation. But then he explained the process of blasting, and that blasting doesn't actually create a hole but more of a mountain of rock, like an eruption. This, of course, translates into—yes, once again having to dig out the foundation, and then remove the rock that had once been in one piece, but would now be in several. Since I didn't have much of a choice, I gave him the okay.

The next day when I visited the site, what was previously marked out as the spot for my home was now just a massive pile of rubble. Since I hadn't borrowed enough to cover blasting and was strapped due to the purchase itself, I had to charge it on my credit card. Luckily my friend, who had done the original digging when the first contractor quit, came along and removed the rock for me at no charge.

But the fun didn't stop there; the same scenario repeated itself when it came time to put in the septic tank. This place was truly a blaster's paradise. Luckily the contractor who got that bid was the same friend who helped me with the foundation. And although we had to blast again, it was only half the price this time and the allocated funds for the initial contractor went to my friend instead.

The credit card company ended up with the best deal—because they were able to charge me a bunch of interest for this unexpected cost!

If I ever had to do it again, I'd be much better prepared, and would make certain there was a little extra in the loan to cover any "incidentals," including the possibility of having to blast.

SURVIVAL HINTS

1. Always try to cover extra costs in your loan whenever possible.
2. Make sure your contractors fully understand the job they are bidding on.
3. Don't worry even when you hit a rock in a hard place—there is always a way around it. I used what was left of mine to build a beauty of a stone wall.

Howdy, Neighbor!

Barbara Amorine

WE DIDN'T MEET our neighbors-to-be right away.

Building our house was quite the task. And living in a place commonly known as "rock haven" meant that every minor detail became a major project. From the start, nothing was easy for us, from putting in the driveway and digging the foundation on through the rest of the job. The attempt to do the driveway ourselves lasted half a day, two inches down through the dirt we went before we hit solid rock. And by solid rock I don't mean a couple of boulders, but a giant rock ledge that filled the entire yard.

This was obviously a job for a professional, and hiring the services of a blaster was our only option. Knowing full well the foundation was going to require more of the same, we went out in search of the best guy to do the job.

There was about a week's delay before the blaster was able to get to our property, which wasn't a problem for our timeline. In the meantime, we visited the lot on many evenings and never saw even a glimpse of our new neighbors from across the street. But we did notice that there were two brand new cars in the driveway, and they also were getting a new roof installed.

Well, the day came for the blasters to arrive, and my husband and I met with them at the property to watch the big explosion. They prepared and planted the explosives, which in a few short minutes would create the space for our new driveway and house.

We were warned to stay out of the way, so we went off down the road to watch from a safe distance. We heard the boss give the go-ahead, followed by a semiloud explosion and a slight rumbling of the ground. Then we watched in horror—as rocks flew into the air and across the road, bouncing relentlessly on and off our future neighbors' brand new cars! While those rocks were still airborne a quick second blast went off, and we again watched in horror as a giant piece of flying sod landed on that same neighbor's brand new roof. We stood aghast, not knowing what to do. Seconds later, we saw the head of the blasting company making a beeline for the neighbors' house.

For the first time since we'd been coming to the property, our new neighbors emerged from their house. From our bird's-eye view down the road, we saw them and the blaster walking around the yard to assess the damage. They all looked upset, but then we saw them shake hands. We slunk away.

As required by law, the blaster was fully insured for this type of disaster. Otherwise, who knows what would have happened. Feeling terrible about the accident, and needing to say something to our future neighbors, we went out and bought a cake, and returned to the site later that day. Cake in hand, we crossed the street. With a three-tap knock on the door, the cake box extended, we held our breath and waited as the door began to slowly open. "Howdy neighbor . . . ," we gulped apologetically. Since then we've become good friends, and whenever we need to liven up a party, we tell the story of how that rock figured prominently in our first encounter.

SURVIVAL HINTS

1. Make sure any and all of your hired contractors are fully insured.
2. Always do the right thing in a difficult situation. Never leave a wrong that you can make right in some way . . . especially with a new neighbor.

Hitting the Highway

Moira Montoya

WHEN WE DECIDED to buy our first house, we were in a mad rush. We had just had a baby and the log cabin we were renting was, to put it mildly, the size of a matchbox. The log cabin was barely big enough for my husband and me—never mind the baby and all the new furniture that comes along with one. It was only a one-bedroom cabin, so her crib had to share the tiny room that held our huge bed. We were cramped and could barely move. To give you a better idea of the size of this cabin, two people could not walk down the hallway at the same time. One would have to wait at one end until the other passed by. Not only that, but the cabin, although I kept it spic and span, always felt dirty to me. I don't know if it was because of a couple of run-ins we had had with some field mice, or just the fact that it was an older cabin; whatever it was, I wanted out—and fast. I didn't want to raise my baby in that dingy dump, so we were eager to get moving on to the new homestead.

The year before our daughter was born, my husband Jerry's parents had given us some land. Now we just needed a house. Since timing was everything to us, we went house shopping for something that would suit our needs and fast. That's when we discovered modular housing. Modular homes look like normal stick-built houses, come in all sizes, and are ready in about half the time compared to building from scratch. We thought that this was exactly the right option for us.

So a modular was the right and speedy solution. Perfect, we thought. Any house that can withstand being driven down the road in sections and at speeds of sixty miles per hour has got to be well built, right? Yes, they are well built, but how well they hold up on the trip really depends on who's driving!

Because of the remote location of our lot, we needed to remove many trees and level the lot before the house could be "planted." We did all this backbreaking work ourselves to save money. And it took forever! But we were on a mission, like most prospective homeowners, and we were excited. The baby would finally have her own bedroom in a clean, mouse-free house. There I'd feel comfortable letting her toys, not to mention her feet, touch the floor.

Life in the rental cabin was getting expensive, too. Our regular rent was $550 a month—a real bargain—but the heat was electric, and this particular log cabin had more cracks and holes in it than rampaging woodpeckers could have made in a decade. It cost us more to heat the place in the winter than to rent it! The bills were piling up while we eagerly awaited the arrival of our new home. Little did we know what was coming instead.

The phone rang one chilly November day. It was the builder. Unfortunately it wasn't good news. Quite the contrary. After stammering a bit, he said:

"I'm sorry to report that there's been an accident."

"Good heavens!" I replied, "was anyone hurt?"

"Well, no *body* was hurt, but some *thing* was. Half your house has fallen off the truck on the interstate!"

"What?" I gasped.

He went on: "They've called in a crane to remove the debris from the highway. You lost your living room and bedroom, unfortunately."

"Oh, my GOD!" I shrieked. What were we going to do now?

He continued: "It's going to be at least another four months for the builder to make a new section to replace it."

My first reaction, after hanging up the phone, was that I hadn't heard him right and that this was just some kind of stalling tactic on his part. Maybe they just didn't have the house ready. Then I got furious. I was mad—

mad as a hatter. Calling my husband to rant and rave about this news only made me angrier. I decided there was no way I was letting this builder get away with burying me any further in rental and energy debt.

I called them back and asked to speak with the manager. I proceeded to tell him which of my bills were now going to be *his* responsibility—until my house was on my land where it belonged, as opposed to being in pieces on the interstate.

Being a gentleman, he kindly told me that these things happened sometimes, and he was sorry but there was nothing else he could do for me. And just to push me over the edge the rest of the way, he added that the company was not responsible for any extra costs to us while we waited—it was all in the fine print, on all those forms we signed. Then I had heard a noise that sounded as if he'd hung up.

"Hello. Hello." I yelled into the phone. "Are you there?"

I couldn't believe it. He had actually hung up on me. Not only was this man *not* going to help me, but now he wasn't even going to talk to me. Or so he thought. But I'm not one to give up that easily.

First things first, I thought to myself. Where in the hell was my manual for my phone? After sifting through my files I located it along with the instructions on how to put a number into speed dial—a feature that I hadn't used before. Once I mastered this task, off to the races I went. I made one call after another. I was not giving in—

until I had an acceptable time frame for the delivery of my house.

For two weeks I called him two to four times a day. Sometimes I just got the receptionist, who would just take my message; other times I actually got through to the manager himself. I knew she was screening his calls, and I finally figured out that if I used different names, the receptionist would put me through directly to him. I've always been able to disguise my voice, so this wasn't a problem. Call after call I made, until the manager finally gave me the answer I was looking for. Our last call went something like this:

"Oh, Hello!" I said. "You *are* in after all."

"Man, how many times are you going to call me?" he asked.

"As many as it takes to get my house delivered," I responded.

"Look, I'm doing everything I can. But I actually have good news," he said.

"What's that?" I replied.

"We're going to put your house ahead of all the others we've got scheduled, and we should be able to get it done in about half the time we originally estimated."

"That's great," I responded. "When can I expect it to be delivered?"

"I can't make you any promises, but you're our top priority," he replied.

In the end, all my ranting, raving, and nagging "persuaded" them to speed-build the missing half of the modular—probably just to get me out of their lives! The delivery ended up happening exactly four weeks from the date of the accident, instead of the original estimate of four months later.

I won't mention the company's name, but their slogan, appropriately enough, was "Only in a Home by . . . ." I don't think even I could have come up with a better slogan for them after everything that happened to us!

SURVIVAL HINTS

1. Always expect and plan for the unexpected when you're building or "planting" a house.
2. Leave yourself enough extra cash to avoid being strapped during an already stressful and sometimes expensive time.
3. If you plan to purchase a modular home, check out the survival rate of the houses the seller transports, and look into cancellation insurance or some way to protect yourself in case the delivery is delayed for any reason.
4. Ask if you can drive the delivery truck yourself!

4

When You're Buying a Condo or Co-op

Moving Up in the World
Ziggy Caruso

My Meeting with the Co-op Board
Elaine Rustick

Sanity Quiz

Your Realtor has taken you to the condo of your dreams. The building has all the amenities you'd hoped for . . . plus some extras, including a neighbor who seems to be going out of his way to make as much noise as possible during your visit. It's the condo you've been waiting for, but the noise is making you nervous.

Do you
A. ignore the racket and sign the papers
B. knock on his door and introduce yourself to get the full perspective
C. tell the Realtor that it's time to move on to another place
D. slam a couple of doors, get the Realtor to drop the price by a couple grand, and start packing

If you answered yes to any of these questions, you need to read on and see how these folks managed with their dilemmas.

Moving Up in the World

Ziggy Caruso

ABOUT FIFTEEN YEARS ago, I decided it was time to invest in a condo. There was an unusual decline in real estate prices in the New York City region because of a bad recession, and I knew it was time to make a move.

I had been making myself cross-eyed reading the real estate ads every day, and had nearly wrecked my car or flattened pedestrians as I drove, gaping, around towns with heavy concentrations of high-rise buildings and all the amenities I hoped to enjoy.

Ruling out towns with too much traffic and pollution, as well as those that didn't have a convenient train line so I could easily get into and out of New York City, where I worked, I finally I settled on a street in the town where I grew up. There, many new buildings had gone up—some of which actually had interesting architectural features—and there was a glut of inventory on the market.

One pair of buildings caught my eye, just as the second one was being completed. I loved how they looked with their huge bay windows and well-kept grounds. I decided to check them out over the coming weekend.

By coincidence, as I bounced home from work on the train midweek, reading the afternoon paper, I saw a big ad for this complex, including the price tag, which was eye-poppingly high. Disappointed, I resigned myself to looking elsewhere, since those condos were way out of my price range.

But as I looked at other apartments, none of them appealed to me. They were all so typically rectangular and the windows were all so small! Why live on a street that had either New York views or vistas of the mountains and have tiny little windows? It made no sense, but there was not much I could do about those boring designs. One Realtor showed me a building on stilts that looked as if it would roll right down the hill where it sat. I imagined it falling right over the cliffs into the Hudson River across the street. Not only that, but it had tiny little rooms and only one tiny closet. Finally, and most unacceptably, it had a dark galley kitchen that was part of the dining room. It was hideous, and there was no way I'd write a check for that place, much to the chagrin of the dagger-nailed Realtor, who did not hide her disdain as I declined to make an offer.

I continued to scour the ads, and to my surprise, a few months later, around Christmas time, I saw in my local paper a notice of an auction at a prestigious condo building. You guessed it—my dream building was having an auction! But then I noticed the date: I was going to be out of town on business, and would miss the big event. Foiled again! I was frustrated, but there was nothing I could do about it. I had no choice but to go and miss the auction.

After I returned from my business trip, having obsessed about the auction the entire five frigid days that I was away, I decided to return to the building that following Saturday to see what I could find out. I walked into the beautiful, sparkling lobby and was greeted immediately by Benny, the cherubic, smiling elderly doorman who had been chatting with a resident, who to my delight was showing the doorman his new little kitten. "A good omen if ever I saw one," I thought. I'm a dedicated cat person, and asked the doorman if they allowed cats. "Of course," he said. "Lots of people have them." I was overjoyed. Now if only there were some condos left.

I next asked about the auction. "Did they sell them all?" I asked.

"No, only a few," he replied. "Go see the people in the sales office and talk to them," he suggested. "It's a nice building and you'd like it here."

Down the hall I went, excited as could be. The saleswoman told me that there were still many apartments to choose from, and she'd be happy to show me the various floor plans and take me to see the different condos. As we went from unit to unit, I was pleased to see the huge windows, the Italian-tile floors, and the large, interesting layouts of the rooms. After seeing every possible layout of the ten offered, I was almost ready to make an offer.

I found out the prices of the various units, and decided on my favorite floor plan. It was a pretty one bedroom overlooking the bucolic tree-lined street facing the mountains. It had an eat-in kitchen separate from the dining room and living room, and a Jacuzzi in the bathroom. The sunlight was streaming in the big, beautiful windows despite the late-December date; it had huge walk-in closets—the most of any floor plan except the penthouse—and was perfect for me. As I walked around on the golden parquet floors, I felt like I'd come home.

I took the saleswoman's card with the price scribbled on the back and told her I'd be back with a check for the deposit, then went home to crunch some numbers to see if I really could afford it. Everything seemed to work, and I returned on Monday with my father, to show him the place. He loved it too, and I was ready to write the check. But that's when I hit a snag.

The saleswoman, a daughter of the developer who'd built the complex, told me that unfortunately the unit I wanted had been turned into a model apartment over the weekend and was no longer available for sale. "Ahhh!" I said. "What am I supposed to do now?"

Frustrated, I asked what else was available, and the saleswoman told me that the unit below the one I liked was still unsold. "Let's go look at it," I replied. When we got to the unit and I looked out the window, I immediately noticed that the ugly building across the street was blocking the mountain/sunset view. This unit was simply on too low a floor!

I asked if any units were available on a higher floor. She said the one above the now model condo was also unsold. Up we sailed on the elevator, and trudged all the way down the hall to the corner apartment. Once inside, I sprinted to the window and fell in love with the view. It was perfect. The view was even better one floor up, and now I was above the tree-line. It was gorgeous, and as my father said, "It's worth the price for this view alone."

Now came the catch. The saleswoman told me that for this unit, the price was actually higher because it was on a higher floor. I rebelled. "I'm not the one who turned the original apartment into a model, and I'm not going paying extra for it. The price you quoted is the most I can afford, and besides, I told you I was coming back with a deposit for that unit."

"Well," she said, "you could talk to my father and see what he says. Do you want me to call him for you?" I agreed, and after she told him about the situation, we had a hilarious conversation that went something like this:

DEVELOPER: "You gotta pay more for the condo because-a it'sa wortha more being ona higher floor."

ME: "But I wanted the lower floor and you made it into a model. Why don't you just move the furniture to a different floor so I can buy the apartment I wanted?"

DEVELOPER: "We donna wanna do that. It'sa too mucha trouble."

ME: "Okay, then I want the one on the next floor."

DEVELOPER: "Why donna you take-a the one below?"

ME: "Because it has an ugly building in the way of the view. I don't want to look at that ugly thing every day that I live here."

DEVELOPER: "Well, ifa you wanna the one up-a-stairs, you gotta pay five thousand more."

ME: "That's outside my budget. I can't do it. If you want to sell it, it has to be for the price I was quoted for the first unit."

DEVELOPER: "I'm already selling these-a below market price—I can'ta do it."

ME: "You already had the auction. You're not going to sell any more of these units right now. We're in a recession and the bottom's out of the market. People are out of work, and you know nobody's buying. Besides, I would have paid your price for the one below, but I can't afford the extra money for this second unit."

DEVELOPER: "[Sigh.] Okay, give me a thousand more than for the one on the floor below and it's a deal."

ME: "Okay," I groaned, "it's a deal."

I wrote the check for the deposit, handed it to the saleswoman, and ran home to start shopping for a mortgage, which was the easy part after negotiating with that developer. But, because the condo was brand new and didn't have 30 percent of the units sold, we all had to put down 25 percent of the price, rather than the customary 5 to 10 percent. It was almost every bit of my savings, but I wasn't backing out at that point.

After all sorts of mix-ups with the mortgage guy, who made one mistake after another with the paperwork, including losing the entire application, getting the amount of the loan wrong, and otherwise driving me and my lawyer crazy with every other thing possible, we set the closing date. At the very last minute, the mortgage company shortchanged my loan by $5,000—the very last little bit left in my seriously depleted savings account. I nearly jumped out my office window—and immediately called my lawyer, a great guy and a good friend. "Calm down," said Bob, "I'll take care of this guy. He just sounds very young and inexperienced, so don't let it get to you."

Naturally Bob was right. He made one last call, everything was straightened out, and the closing went on as scheduled. We drove to the appointment and entered the sleek cool lobby of the elegant offices of the developer's attorney, then whooshed up the elevator to the top floor. I held my breath along with all my paperwork, my cashier's check, and copies of every other scrap of paper that had been involved—just in case anything else had been lost.

Finally we were seated in the plush and paneled conference room, where we shook hands with the lawyer and the developer, who in person was courtly and polite. After signing my name about 4,000 times, everything was done. My lawyer grinned at me and said, "Well, kid, you did it!" I rolled my eyes and thanked him for all his help and for saving what was left of my sanity, not to mention my savings account.

I suppose I could tell you about packing and moving, but it was boring and uneventful so I'll spare you the details. It's enough to say that on the first and, I might add, hottest day of that summer, I moved into my windowed palace above the trees. And despite having more boxes than furniture for quite a long time, I truly was happy to be a homeowner at last—and just in time for the opening of the pool!

SURVIVAL HINTS

1. Sometimes you have to keep what you want in mind to eventually get it, even if it seems like a long shot.

2. Don't give up, even if there are obstacles, because sometimes a little compromise goes a long way when you're negotiating.

My Meeting with the Co-op Board

Elaine Rustick

A FEW YEARS ago, I wanted to move from my small studio in a garden apartment complex to a larger one bedroom in a luxury high-rise co-op building in Fort Lee, New Jersey. It was a great location, close to the George Washington Bridge, which made for easy travel in and out of New York City, and it also had a pretty park across the street. It was a much larger space than before, and I was excited about the move.

But first I had to go through the meeting with the dreaded co-op board. Now, I'd heard all kinds of horror stories about all the bizarre things that can happen at those meetings, where clashes of egos can kill your chances of being admitted, where tempers may flare over almost nothing, and people's future residential bliss may hang in the balance of whimsy and the mood of the moment.

Cooperatives are a specific type of community, one in which a buyer purchases shares of ownership in the building, and they have many more rules about who can live there, as well as the financial requirements for that individual that must be met in order to qualify. For example, there are rules about how much money a buyer can borrow when purchasing a co-op, but this isn't the case with a condo. Unlike a condominium, in which the buyer obtains an apartment or unit but only owns what's inside the walls of that unit, in a co-op, the buyer obtains shares in the entire building. Everyone owns a portion of the whole, and becomes responsible for shares of the underlying mortgage for the entire building, along with utilities, maintenance of the building, and property taxes, rather than for just their apartment. Consequently, the "maintenance charge" for a co-op is much higher than in a condo.

Condo sales prices are higher, and all the other charges must be paid separately, including utilities, taxes, mortgage, and maintenance, usually referred to as an association fee, and there are many fewer rules for condo owners than for co-op owners. On the plus side for co-ops, the sales price can be significantly lower, as much as half that of a condo. But once it's all added up side by side, the expenses usually end up being comparable for both.

As I mentioned earlier, co-op boards have many more rules about everything compared to condos, including pet ownership; visitors; who can move in; subletting for how long, to whom, and when; smoking; quiet hours; renovations; where visitors may park, for how long, and when; registration of vehicles; and many other policies and regulations. These rules are subject to change upon a vote by the members of the co-op, and then all the members must abide by them.

I had heard all kinds of peculiar stories about co-op board meetings in which the applicant's paperwork was in perfect order, credentials were spotless, and all seemed to be as clearly a go as could be. But then there would be this one innocent little question that, when answered incorrectly, would shoot down the entire deal. Those were usually run-of-the-mill questions, but they can also run to the fanciful, such as, "Do you plan to do surgery in your apartment?" "Will you be adopting and housing stray animals?" "Does your entire extended family expect to live with you?" Answering any of these in the affirmative would probably be the end of the line for you!

Having heard every frightful detail of friends' and acquaintances' nightmare experiences with these co-op boards, I was nervous about passing muster with this august body. But I'd come this far, had filled out all of what felt like 187 forms, had gone through the usual ordeal of arranging financing, and had dealt with all the other details of buying a home. This stamp of approval was the last link in the chain of my future and hopefully happy homeownership. So off I went, dressed to the nines, every hair and eyelash in place, to meet with the dreaded co-op board.

First I was introduced, and there they all sat, an owlish bunch, each one more elderly than the last. How much trouble could they possible be? They all looked like my grandparents! And before them sat copies of all my financial records—my entire financial history, as it were—to be read and discussed, laid bare for the co-op board as required to be approved to buy shares in the co-op. This scrutiny exists because the board wants to be sure that anyone admitted can afford to live there, but it seemed strange having my entire financial life laid bare before this elderly tribunal.

They carefully reviewed the paperwork once more, turning pages slowly and silently while I sweated, both inwardly and in fact. I wondered if the old guy on the left had actually nodded off, when at last the eldest of the gray eminences cleared his throat and asked with a scowl if I'd read and understood the rules of the entire twenty-five-page co-op rule book or had questions about any of it.

Thinking that I'd never seen so many rules about so many tiny little details in my whole life, I replied that yes, I understood it all, but I had a question. Now, I'd been dreading asking it, but there really was no way around it. I took a deep breath. This, I decided, was probably the moment of doom for the future of my co-op purchase. I said, as bravely as I could:

"I saw in the rules that it says no animals. I have this cat. I inherited her from my late husband."

"Ah!" he said, scowling at me over the top of his half-glasses and turning up his hearing aide.

I waited for the verdict, my heart beginning to pound.

"We'll pretend we never heard." He didn't even crack a smile until I did. Okay, one hurdle jumped, what next?

"So you are a social worker at a hospital?" another asked, her glasses slipping a little to one side.

"Yes, I work in the psychiatry department," I said, modestly.

"How lovely. You must be a very smart and kind-hearted lady," said the most grandmotherly of the group. She looked like she belonged on the label of a box of oatmeal cookies. I smiled at her. She was probably thinking that I'd come in handy as they all became even more decrepit and needed a helping hand at the front door, not that I'd ever be home with my hours!

Next I heard a clearing of a throat as a quavering voice said, "Well, if there are no other questions for Mrs. R, we'll proceed to the vote." This from the gentleman who obviously had the most seniority, probably having been born during the first Roosevelt administration—and I mean Teddy, not FDR!

I was ushered out of the room to wait. Rolling my eyes as I looked out the window at the beautiful park across the street, I hoped my poor little cat wouldn't be held against me, despite how it seemed to go when I'd mentioned her, and I hoped I'd made a saintly enough impression as a family therapist to squeak past any other objections.

After about five minutes of quiet suspense—all I could hear was murmuring behind the door—they asked me to return to my hot seat before the panel. I held my breath and let the fates take over.

"Mrs. Elaine Rustick, we are delighted to approve you, and welcome to the Majestic Towers. We are pleased to have such a wonderful new neighbor, and look forward to seeing you at our next general business meeting!"

Miraculously, they voted to approve me unanimously, cat and all, and apparently this was a rare occurrence for the board. And so Misty and I moved to our tower and enjoyed our view for the next ten years, proving that not all co-op boards are difficult, no matter what you may have otherwise heard.

PART 2: STAYING SANE WHEN YOU'RE SELLING A HOME

5

When Selling Is Boggling Your Mind

Sanity Quiz

Your Realtor has brought a young newlywed couple in to see your home. Just then a bathroom pipe bursts. It's not a big hole, but a little pinhole with a constant stream of water that is now slowly filling your vanity.

Do you
A. shove a bunch of towels under there to absorb the water and hope they don't look inside
B. make believe you are doing your morning bathroom visit and refuse to let them in
C. quickly chew up a piece of gum and stick it to the hole in hopes that it will outlast their viewing
D. tell them what happened and that you are going to fix it promptly

If you picked A, B, or C, then you need help! Read on to see the kinds of jams our contributors found themselves in!

No Longer Sane

Tom Pritchard

SINCE I AM no longer allowed to possess sharp objects, I'm writing this with a blue crayon, a task made even more challenging because my sleeves are sewn shut and strapped behind my back. Consequently, my advice will be pretty pithy.

As you've probably surmised, sanity-maintenance eluded me after fifty grueling weeks of being what Realtors like to call a "motivated seller" (a dreadful misnomer since all I sold during that ordeal were stocks, bonds, and my treasured 1955 Brooklyn Dodger memorabilia, a relentless dispersal prompted by Realtor-mandated "improvements" to the property). Two weeks short of a year and tens of thousands of dollars later, I went to the closing. Given what the buyers offered for my house, a more appropriate gathering would have been an arraignment, since their offer

constituted grand larceny. So when they insisted that I remove the brand-new, custom-made, designer bedroom
draperies, which had cost me many sleepless nights and
thousands of dollars. I leapt across the table and . . . tried
to choke the buyer.

And that's why I'm here at Heavenly Hills trying to
scratch out my life's lessons with a blunt crayon behind
my back. To avoid a similar fate, you might want to consider my advice.

Realtors

Clean up your joint as best you can, and then invite four
to five recommended Realtors to do a market evaluation. Importantly, you should do your own evaluation
using comps (comparable sales) from Multiple Listing
Service (MLS) before meeting with the agents. Focus on
recent *sales* and not listings. Then sit down with the
agents, armed with your own research.

Getting a Realtor's license is no easy task. First off,
they have to spend a great deal of time in classes, learn-
ing how to pencil in the three blanks on a preprinted
listing agreement and the four blanks on a purchase
agreement. Next, classes on how to operate a key lockbox. These grueling exercises can consume a ton of
effort and time—in some cases as long as a whole week!
And if that weren't enough, then they have to spend *another* whole week at Glamour Shots Inc. getting just the
right smiling headshot for their four-color business cards.

Which reminds me: There must be a correlation between prolonged use of Crest whitening strips and impaired math skills. Every Realtor I dealt with had difficulties in this regard. The first one measured my house and came up 400 square feet short of the actual measurements. Apparently she decided that the living room and the family room didn't count. Even more disturbing were the math skills of my second Realtor, who overstated how much the house would sell for by almost $10,000! But I digress.

Agents must have a highly developed skill set. For starters, they must be able to identify a bathroom and to quickly distinguish that room from the kitchen. They must have a cell phone with an irritatingly distinctive ring tone, like the sound of "wispy winds" or "babbling brook." And lastly, they must know the trendiest assortment of deli meats, pasta salads, and whole-grain rolls for the Broker Open House. And equally important, they must know precisely how much food to order, so that when the homeowner returns, there will be but a single parsley sprig, a dollop of curried mayo, and a limp leaf of lettuce on the platter for him to feast on.

Other skills include crafting a marketing program for under a hundred bucks. This requires the ability to create newspaper ads three lines long, since "big ads with a photo of the house don't work." Realtors must think that three-line ciphers—3BR/2B HWF WBF 1flFR—that can be understood only by the National Security Agency and New York apartment seekers is the better way. Or maybe, just maybe, they are advocates of three-liners because they have to pay for the ads with their own money—YIKES! In any event, Realtors are a necessary evil and a better option than walking in front of your house wearing a sandwich board. Then again . . .

A word about FSBOs (For Sale by Owner). The FSBO option, using a discount broker (1 percent fee for getting you on MLS and a cardboard sign in front of your palace), is an option to consider after six months, because by then, all the Realtor's marketing efforts will have run their course. As such, going to a discount broker for 1 percent and dropping your price equal to the selling agent's commission might be worth considering.

Speaking of commissions, don't pay 6 or 7 percent unless you need a bush plane to show the property. Depending on the market, 4 to 5 percent will get you an agent. Before signing, get a written marketing plan with *specifics*, for example, ads, open houses, color brochures for buyers to take home after a showing, and Web site listings beyond MLS (sites like Realtor.com).

Insist on a weekly written report to include number of previews, number of showings and second showings, and new listings and sales in the neighborhood. In this regard, make sure to preview your competition. Put yourself in the buyers' shoes. Know the market and the competition—you are not selling in a vacuum. And in a slower market, many buyers are taking their time and looking at *everything* on the market.

Pricing

You'd think that setting a listing price would be easy. Not so. Even with a five-foot stack of comps, sellers overvalue their homes. It reminds me of the George Carlin bit about all the "stuff" he has and treasures. And when he packs all of his stuff to go visit a friend, he then has to move their "shit" to make room for his stuff. Obviously, the bit is far funnier than the synopsis, but the point is clear. Sellers have problems being objective. So remember these old saws: It is better to sell and regret than to keep and regret—a popular post facto rant of dot-com investors. And my father's favorite: Pigs get fat, and hogs get slaughtered.

Use all of the market evaluations you received, consider recent sales, hold your nose, and set an attractive, competitive price. Then be prepared to drop the price 5 percent after thirty showings or sixty days, whichever comes first. You must be aggressive with pricing and make meaningful drops to attract and motivate buyers.

Okay, now the house is on the market and you start to get showings. And showings lead to an insatiable desire for *feedback*!

Feedback

Sellers yearn for buyer feedback. This feedback, however, is usually unreliable and frequently misleading. Most comments are designed to thwart debate or to spare the seller's feelings, especially when the buyer's issue is not fixable. (Who's going to tell you your house is butt ugly and your neighborhood is one pizza box short of a landfill?)

If you really want the unvarnished truth about what buyers think of your precious home, plant a voice-activated micro recorder on each level. Available at Radio Shack for twenty bucks, they are worth every penny because, when it comes to feedback, buyers are liars. However, if you listen in when they think they're alone, you get to hear real feedback—which, although it might put you on the defensive and leave you feeling vulnerable, might also tell you wonderful things about your house that you can use to your advantage! It never hurts to know what a buyer really thinks!

Today's Buyers

Today's buyers want turnkey properties with all the HGTV trendoid trimmings that have the longevity of a moth, like black or stainless steel appliances, and designer options that will smack of green shag carpets and avocado appliances within months.

I decided not to update my kitchen, believing that the new owner would want to make their own decorative choices. Plus I didn't want to shell out $40,000 to a contractor who would never show up, cut corners, and lie to me while doing a lousy job that would come in over the bid and months late. That whole scenario would also include enriching a defense attorney (to help with the homicide charges!), so I opted out on the kitchen makeover. But when two lesser houses with re-modeled kitchens sold instantly *on my block*, I realized that the kitchen makeover might be a necessary conces-sion given today's buyers. Luckily I didn't have to go there.

Speaking of buyers, there is one hopelessly incapable, nonhandy cluster of individuals out there. These buyers might be draped in digital apparatus, yet need an opera-tor's manual to use a screwdriver. They have six-figure incomes, yet need to use their platinum Visa at the drive-through. They have phones that play movies, make movies, reset their thermostat, and start their cars, but they are a month behind on the bill. This type of buyer has the income to qualify for a mortgage and the money-management skills of a hamster—make that a hamster with a gambling problem.

Bottom line: They can buy your house, but nothing more. And with tradesmen like electricians, plumbers, and carpenters charging the same hourly rate as attor-neys, buyers scurry from house to house looking for the perfect home, one that requires zero work and zero in-vestment after the close.

Survival Tools

I keep forgetting that this is one of those "How To" books and not the Gospel according to Tom, so I'd better pass on a few helpful hints before the editor kicks out the whole chapter.

PODS and iPods

The two most important tools in your sanity-maintenance kit will be PODS and iPods.

PODS.   Portable On Demand Storage (PODS) containers are storage units that are delivered to your home. They sit on the ground and have a roll-up door for easy access. The ceiling is opaque fiberglass and acts like a skylight, so it's easy to load and arrange stuff. They come in two sizes—get the bigger 16 x 8 x 8 foot unit. The PODS container is used initially to declutter your house for viewing. Fill the container with oversized furniture, closet clutter, garage clutter, and packed boxes (if you've started that dreaded task).

Next to the PODS container should be a Dumpster. This is for the junk you don't need, don't like, don't use, don't fit into, and won't sell at your tag sale, like Tupperware bowls with no lids, khakis with a thirty-two-inch waist, that blanket with a "small hole" in it. Be disciplined. Remember, what you don't toss must be packed, shipped, unpacked, and then stuck into another space-consuming spot in your new digs.

Once you've filled the PODS container and the Dumpster, the units will be hauled away, one to storage and one to the dump. After you sell your house, the company will return your PODS container just in time for your Moving Sale. Empty the container and then fill it with items you are NOT selling, items that you will be taking with you. This way, you can consolidate the rest of your Not for Sale items in a few rooms. (PODS containers can also be used as a guest cottage for visiting in-laws—the one-call-for-haul-away feature comes in handy here.) PODS are wonderful!

iPods.   I must have taken my dog for several hundred walks since I had to vacate the premises whenever there was a showing. I would spot the buyer and Realtor pulling up to the curb, grab my iPod, hook up my dog, Annie, and scamper out the back door. Then we'd walk to the park and back. If the car was still there after the fifteen-minute walk, that would be a good sign. Buyers with no interest are usually in and out in ten minutes. So if I returned and saw the car still parked in front, I would hide in my neighbor's shrubs and listen to my iPod. Then when the buyers exited the house, I would strain to hear any comments. (And at that critical moment, of course, a truck would thunder by or a jet would roar overhead and obliterate all but "I agree totally"!)

The most memorable episode occurred one morning when a fancy new red Honda pulled up in front. Annie and I dashed out the back door. When we returned from the park, the red Honda was still parked in front. I hid in the bushes, plugged in my iPod and waited. Another twenty minutes passed, and I was getting very excited. I was also getting very wet as the April skies dumped buckets. I ignored the rain dripping from my nose. All I could think was that they had been in the house for over an hour! They had to be interested.

Another thirty minutes ticked by. They are writing up an offer! All cash deal! No contingencies! My expectations grew and so did the rains. I was just sharing my conclusions with Annie, when my neighbor from across the street dashed from his house, jumped into the red Honda, and drove off. I looked down at Annie and discovered, for the first time, that golden retrievers are capable of glaring! We emerged from the bushes and slunk home. I got the silent treatment for hours.

My crayon is down to a tiny nub, but I have just enough left to debunk the biggest fallacy in the entire realm of real estate: the St. Joseph myth.

If your house doesn't sell in the first eleven minutes after the listing pops up on MLS, someone will suggest that you bury a statue of St. Joseph in your backyard. Importantly, you must bury St. Joseph upside down, head first, into the ground. Once they have repeated these instructions several times, they will bore you to death with several success stories (all urban myths, I suspect) about sellers having their house on the market for seven years, and twenty minutes after planting St. Joseph, they sell the house for twice the listing price, all in gold bullion, dropped off the next day.

I heard this tale from dozens of believers and toyed with the idea. I went to Mass on Sunday and prayed: "St. Joseph, how about I spare you the indignity of being buried in the dirt in exchange for sending a buyer my way. Amen." After another month passed, I concluded that St. Joseph had a dirt fetish, so I obliged and planted him, head first, in my backyard. I looked down at the statue, looking like a patient in a proctologist's chair and sighed, "Whatever."

Six months passed without a sale, so I concluded what any sane person would have: St. Joseph is no longer into real estate. Like all the other clever people, he got out before the bubble burst.

SURVIVAL HINTS

1. Paint your front door and threshold, and get a new mat.
2. Rekey the front-door lock so that the door opens effortlessly with one hand. This makes it easy for Realtors to get in and show the house.
3. Make sure to leave music, air conditioners, or fans running to kill the dead silence as well as to mask sounds from outside.
4. Clean windows inside and out, leave blinds and curtains open, and put 100-watt bulbs in all your lamps and fixtures.
5. Attach a box of flyers to your For Sale sign. It also helps to attach helium balloons to the sign each week when there's an open house.

6. After thirty days, offer a cash bonus of between one and two thousand dollars to the *buyer's* agent. That will almost double their cut, since they have to split their base commission.
7. Change your MLS wording every other Thursday so your ad will sound fresh as agents and buyers are planning their weekend house hunting.
8. Rewrite the descriptive copy, add a bonus or benefit such as, "Close to schools, park, etc."
9. Hold an open house every other weekend (tied to the MLS copy changes).

The Real Estate Agent from Hell

Sammy Woods

BUYING OR SELLING real estate is always a stressful affair. If you have a decent real estate agent, however, it can mean the difference between mild stress, which is more like "excitement" than anything else, and the intense stress that's normally associated with what I call the "the double V"—popping valium and consuming vodka like the Taliban is firing scud missiles at your front door . . . in the middle of an earthquake.

Many years back, I was trying to sell a condo in Hoboken, New Jersey, when the real estate market for condos in Sinatra's and baseball's birthplace had hit rock bottom. A friend of mine recommended a local real estate agent to help me market my place, so I called her and set up a meeting. Her name was Janet. She arrived about twenty minutes late, reeking of perfume, and with more pashminas flying in her wake than American flags at a used car lot on the Fourth of July. Janet was about fifty at the time and elegant, but not entirely there, if you catch my drift.

"Sam, this space is mag*nif*icent!" she exclaimed. "Buyers will *love* the tall windows, high ceilings, and hardwood floors. Yes. Yes. Yes. We *must* do business together." Like many in her profession, Janet, I thought, had a flair for the dramatic. We agreed upon an asking price and I signed a sixty-day contract for her to act as my agent. Janet went to work immediately, recommending that I put most of my furniture in storage to make my one-bedroom home appear larger. I complied. Then she recommended a coat of paint. I complied. She recommended I repair a few broken tiles. I complied.

Janet arranged a few showings, but no dice, no one was interested in buying. I thought maybe the price she suggested was a bit high, but she insisted it was on the money. "Sam, the problem is *not* the price, my dear," she said as dramatically as Kathleen Turner in a 1980s potboiler. "The problem is the *decor!* You *must* let my friend Natasha redecorate your place! It will bring out the *inner* beauty of this absolutely *divine* space!"

Oh, brother, I thought to myself, this is going to start getting expensive. I hemmed and I hawed, but after several more weeks of no buyer surfacing, I decided to meet with the designer. Natasha, it turned out, was a top-to-toe Janet clone, with the exception of the hair color (Janet was bottle-auburn, Natasha bottle-black). After an hour of Natasha running all around exclaiming that I *must* buy Stickley this and Ming that, I'd had about enough. Since I wasn't planning a run on Fort Knox, I knew I was going to have to show Natasha the door.

"You cannot throw *me* out. I am Natasha! I have done interior design for—" said Natasha, as I let the door close in her face. Whew. Dodged a bullet there. The next day, Janet was furious with me.

"You can't throw out *Natasha!*" she said haughtily.

"Listen, Janet," I said. "The sixty days is about up and I'm thinking you and I should part company."

"You cannot throw *me* out. I am Janet! I have sold homes for—" said Janet, as I let the door close in her face. Whew again.

"I'm finally rid of this drama queen," I thought to myself.

And then it started—the nightmare. Janet began to call and leave messages on my home machine and at my office day and night. At first, the calls merely chastised me for my folly in actually thinking that I would ever sell my place without her. Then they started to get, well, a bit unhinged. The messages, none of which I returned, began to get more bizarre and rambling. "Sam, it's just . . . I can't begin . . . I don't know, why, well . . . Perhaps, no . . . It's just, well, not really . . . Hee-hee! Sam, are you there?"

Then the tone of the messages changed. They went from incoherent to coldly lucid and irate. "Sam, I know you're there. Pick up that phone! I will *not* be ignored!" I thought I could live with a few nutty phone calls, but then things took a turn for the worse.

I came home from work and there were yellow Post-it notes around my apartment pointing out all the reasons why my place wouldn't sell! There was a nail hole in the kitchen wall that hadn't been properly spackled. The fridge was too small. The curtain in the bathroom was the wrong shade of blue. You couldn't bounce a quarter on the bed spread. You get the idea.

Just when I thought I had noticed all of the craziness, I walked over to my fish tank. The aquarium heater had been turned all the way up and my finned friends were now bouillabaisse.

I called an all-night locksmith and had the locks changed. The next night I left my office in Manhattan and there was Janet, pacing up and down on the sidewalk waiting for me. "Sam, who do *you* think you are?!" she screamed. I'd seen the movie *Fatal Attraction,* so I figured I had better get the hell out of there. I ran about a block with Janet in pursuit. I was able to get into a cab and get the door closed just as this nut-job came running up. "You can't leave me standing in the middle of *Fifth Avenue* like this!" she screamed as my cab sped off.

A couple of gallons of scotch and a restraining order later, I was finally able to put the whole thing behind me.

My next real estate agent was a ringer for the nice little old man in the old TV commercial who said, "Pepperidge Farm remembers!" I sold my condo, moved to the 'burbs, and believe you me, the next move I make will be out of *this* house in a pine box!

Did You Miss Us?

Ginny Chandoha

MY HUSBAND AND I spent ten years transforming our 1960s ranch-style home into a modern contemporary. We used top-of-the-line materials and did most of the work ourselves because most contractors couldn't or wouldn't spend the time we required to make things as close to perfect as was humanly possible. We had building code inspections every step of the way, obtaining all the necessary permits and certificates of occupancy required. Not only did we meet code, we usually exceeded it.

The changes we made were not only to our taste, but also with an eye on what house hunters demanded in a home. I had been a Realtor myself at one time, and knew how to make my home appealing to the buying public. When the time came to sell, we enlisted a highly respected Realtor. Our agent began talking up our house, generating a great deal of interest throughout the real estate community in the gem about to come onto the market.

In our area, a seller was required to leave a home neat and tidy for showing. I made sure my home was spotless. The floors sparkled with a new finish, the walls gleamed with fresh, neutral paint, all hardware had been replaced with shiny new brass, the wood paneling down-stairs had been cleaned and polished, new carpeting installed. Even the old driveway had been ripped up and replaced with new asphalt. The kitchen appliances and countertops were new. The roof had been replaced only a couple of years earlier, right down to the rafters, and architectural shingles were used. All doors and windows were replaced with top-of-the-line materials. The interior of the house looked like a photo out of *Architectural Digest*. The exterior was also carefully groomed. I'd spent many an hour landscaping the nearly one-acre parcel with plantings native to the area. A natural stone path meandered through the variety of blooming flowers and shrubs. Our home glowed with pride of ownership, and our hope was that the next owners would love it as much as we had.

When the For Sale sign went up, a nonstop parade of prospective buyers traipsed through. Only one day elapsed before we received our first full-price offer. We were ecstatic. But wait! There was another offer, and another! A full-fledged bidding war ensued. We were offered more than we'd ever dreamed possible for our house. We were anxious to leave the area, and after a few days decided to halt the bidding and award the contract to the original bidders at the then-highest bid. We'd met them briefly when they had toured the property, were convinced they loved the house for the same reasons we did, and that it would be left in good hands.

At first, everything went smoothly. An inspector spent several hours carefully examining every aspect of the house. Even though the bones of the house were thirty years old, the rest of it was new, and we not only had records of all materials we'd used to upgrade the house, but we'd taken detailed photographs at every step of the rehabilitation. I was able to show the inspector the interiors of the walls, floors, and roof as they were being rebuilt. I could tell him in great detail how we'd gotten our homeowner's electrical license, what gauge wiring we'd used, and how we'd had two wiring inspections (rough, and then finished). Needless to say, our home passed with flying colors prior to both parties signing the residential contract of sale. According to the contract's mortgage contingency, the buyers had to place in escrow a 10 percent down payment of the agreed-upon sale price upon signing the contract, and then had forty-five days to obtain a written commitment from an institutional lender. We were assured that financing would be no problem.

While we waited for the buyers to get their financing in place, we rented a moving van and emptied the house of all contents except a few items we'd need when we returned for the closing—so few things, we'd be able to toss them into the back of the truck, hand over the house keys, say good-bye to that chapter in our lives, and begin a new one in New Hampshire.

Things were going well until I got a call from our lawyer, Al. The buyers' attorney wanted us to get certificates of occupancy approval for the downstairs woodstove, the shed, the back deck, and the fence separating our property from our neighbors, most of which we'd added to the existing house during our years of renovation. Certificates of occupancy were required by the town we lived in, and were proof that everything built or installed was within the property boundary lines, had been inspected, and had met or exceeded the town's building codes. These certificates had to be obtained prior to the sale of a house, and were transferable to a new owner.

I knew my stuff. The downstairs woodstove was grandfathered in. If anyone had bothered to read the detailed list of completion dates we'd provided, they would have seen that the woodstove had been installed prior to the town's requirement for permits, inspections, or certification. Regarding the shed, the town only required permits, certification, and taxes paid on sheds larger than one hundred square feet. Ours was ninety-six square feet, and well within the property line. The back deck was a "floating" deck, meaning it was not attached to the house, had no footings, and rested on what was formerly a brick patio. It was also less than a foot above the ground, and didn't require railing or certification. As for the fence between properties, it had been there when we had moved into the house twenty-five years earlier, and had been erected by the previous neighbors. I informed Al that the fence did not belong to us. The nit-picking by the buyers was really starting to irritate me.

I was even less happy with them when we had to post-pone the closing twice because they couldn't get financing. After three months of waiting, the closing was supposed to be held in two weeks, and we thought every-thing had been settled. But no. Another call about the fence. This time the buyers wanted to have the property surveyed. Al, who was slow to boil, was becoming increas-ingly agitated. He advised them that they'd had plenty of time to have all the tests, surveys, or whatever else they wanted conducted prior to signing the contract. Enough was enough! Without our permission, they went ahead with a survey anyway. The fence was within the neigh-bor's property line, except at the very end. The fence veered slightly so that a couple of inches of our land were on their side of the fence. No big deal. No reason to cause hard feelings among friendly neighbors. It would be easy enough to move, if anyone really cared. In twenty-two years, we'd never had a need to demand those two inches be returned to us. I laughed derisively when the buyers wanted to know if we'd ever had any al-tercation with the neighbors about the fence.

I kept hoping these morons' financing would fall through so we could put the house back on the market. I didn't feel these people deserved such a great house, or our equally fine neighbors. Our real estate agent assured us the market was still hot and our house would sell quickly, at the price of our last offer. Alas, the buyers had gotten their financing, and the closing was scheduled to proceed.

I felt such animosity toward these people that I couldn't stand to have them in the same room, much less sitting right across the table. So the weekend before the closing, we drove down to our old neighborhood to have Sunday breakfast with Al and his wife, and to sign the power of attorney so our presence wouldn't be required at the closing.

The buyers had been apprised of our weekend stay at what was still our house. There was nothing left in it except a mattress on the floor, a small TV, and a pot or pan for us to cook a meal with. We used disposable paper plates and plastic forks. For chairs we used the deck furniture, which we were including with the house. Also included were all the brass woodstove utensils, the old dehumidifier for the downstairs, all appliances, including washer and dryer, microwave, dishwasher, stove, and two refrigerators. I'd also left a folder that included the manuals for everything in the house.

The house was stuffy from being closed up, so we turned on the dehumidifier. It hadn't been used in awhile, and gave off a foul odor. We weren't about to clean it for these ingrates, so we put it out in the shed. The following morning we showered, and left our cat, Oreo, sleeping on the mattress. We spent a fun morning with Al and his wife, and around noon headed back to the house to pack up the last of our belongings, bid our neighbors good-bye, and close the book on that period of our lives. We'd spent many wonderful years in that house. It was going to be sad packing the truck with the last remnants of our life there.

The first thing we noticed when we got back to the house was that Oreo was missing. We frantically searched the entire house for him. It's hard for a cat to hide in an empty house. The closets were bare, the rooms vacant. How could he have disappeared? My husband finally found Oreo cowering under the oil tank in the furnace room. We couldn't fathom what had frightened him so. Then I noticed that the neat folder of appliance manuals was disorganized and rifled through, and called it to my husband's attention. He noticed that the remote controls for the central air conditioning were out of their wall mounts. We also noted that the lockbox on the front door was missing. "Someone's been in the house while we were gone!" he exclaimed.

I called the real estate agency and demanded to know who had been in the house while we were out. Knowing full well that we'd be there, the buyers had chosen that weekend to do a walk-through. A walk-through is usually done hours before a closing, not days in advance, and certainly not when the rightful owners are occupying the

house! I felt humiliated! We'd left our clothing, our toiletries, and our personal items out in full view of what
I'd presumed would be our eyes only. During the entire
closing process, I had gone from mildly annoyed to extremely irritated with these people. Now I was downright
furious! The nerve! We couldn't wait to be packed, back
in New Hampshire, and done with them forever.

We were almost ready to pull out of the driveway
when the telephone rang. It was Al, stating that the buyers had done a walk-through while we were at his house.
They accused us of *stealing* the dehumidifier! What an in-
sult! Not only were we *giving* them the dehumidifier, but
the air in New Hampshire is extremely dry, and not only
didn't we want the ancient thing, we certainly didn't
need to steal it! I told Al that if the buyers had bothered
to look in the shed when they'd invaded our space, they
would have seen the damn thing!

Their second complaint was that they'd turned on
the water in the shower and it was only a trickle. Now
these idiots wanted to have the town water department
perform a water pressure test. *What!?* We'd both taken
showers that morning, and nothing was unusual. I told
Al to wait while I turned on the shower, the tub and sink
faucets, and flushed the toilet. All was normal, and I told
him so. Besides, the water pressure had been tested during the full house inspection, and had passed without
hesitation. These people were certifiably crazy! Al
heaved a sigh and said he'd get back to me. Cursing, I
slammed down the phone. I was beyond angry! Beyond

livid! I was spitting mad! We threw the last of our belongings into the truck and sped back to New Hampshire.

The very next afternoon I received an excited call from our Realtor. The water pressure test had been performed and the pressure was deemed below normal. The water pressure valve would have to be replaced by a licensed plumber, to the tune of at least $150. I couldn't believe it. I called the town water department. The engineer pulled our file and said that our water pressure was only slightly below the normal range. I asked if it was an unusual reading for a house thirty years old. He said that all the houses on the street were the same age, and if they were tested, they'd have the same reading, or worse. I was further advised that the pressure reading was actually quite remarkable, considering the age of the house. I was stunned when the engineer went on to say that he strongly opposed replacing the valve because it was solid brass, whereas the newer ones are plastic, don't last very long, and need frequent replacing. I was shocked when he said that unless the water didn't run at all, to keep the valve we had, and, in essence, do nothing. If it ain't broke, don't fix it. I asked for his name, took his number, and related this information verbatim to Al. If the buyers wanted to replace the valve, they were free to do so when they took possession of the house. I was glad we weren't attending the closing because I knew I'd be arrested for murder.

It was the morning of the closing, and there was yet another, last-minute demand. The damn fence! They wanted to fax us affidavits, attesting that we'd never been denied access to our two inches of property, and had never had an incident with our neighbors. They threatened to halt the closing if we didn't sign and immediately fax back the paperwork. I was tempted to tell them to shove those affidavits where the sun didn't shine and put the house back on the market, but at that point, we just wanted it all over with so we could move into our gorgeous home in the mountains. We signed on the dotted line, and the closing commenced without further ado.

Our former neighbors kept us apprised of the new owners. After all they'd put us through, they never moved into the house. It was nothing to them except an investment. When we visited the area four years later, we were shocked by the condition of the property. Trees had not been trimmed and choked out the sunlight. The flowers and shrubs I'd lovingly planted were overgrown with weeds. There was still the welcome mat we'd left behind, the interior of the house unchanged from the way we'd left it, from what we could see through dirty windows. However, there was one major difference. The house looked dejected, so devoid of life. I was nearly in tears as I put my hand on the home we'd lovingly restored, and whispered, "Have you missed us?" The second surprise was the For Sale sign. We'd heard through the grapevine the buyers were getting divorced. What goes around comes around.

The house was sold again, and the buyers from hell tried to pass off all the hard work we'd put into the house as their own, but our former neighbors set the new owners straight. And now the flowers bloom once again, and the house basks in the love of its new caretakers. Their first child was born a few months ago. We're happy that there is new life in our old house.

SURVIVAL HINTS

1. Keep careful records of everything that's done to your home, with dates and prices included.
2. Know the laws that govern zoning, building codes, etc., and be sure to get all the necessary permits and have all inspections done as scheduled. Otherwise, when you go to sell your home, there can be big problems with your local building inspectors!
3. Remember that no matter how much you may like your buyers, it's still a business transaction and it's best to keep things on a formal basis until after the sale goes through.
4. Don't be thrown by unexpected requests, unreasonable demands, and other obstacles from the buyer. Sometimes it's inexperience, and other times it's just insanity!

Selling Stupidity

Susan Berlin

IT WAS THE mid-1980s, and we were selling our house in Brooklyn, New York, to move on up to the suburbs. In the course of telling our plans to our friends, family, and acquaintances, our former day-care provider offered to buy our house. We considered this couple very trustworthy, as they had cared for our most valuable commodity, our firstborn (and at the time, only) child. But we were *really* stupid!

We settled on a price and, because we really had no connections, we contacted a lawyer recommended by the buyer—our first mistake. I said we were stupid, and also young and too inexperienced to know that it is never a good idea for the seller to obtain the services of a lawyer who is a friend of the buyer! It clearly was a conflict of interest, at the very least, and we ended up getting the short end of the stick, because although the lawyer represented us, his friendship with the other couple ultimately took precedence.

Having never sold a house before and being naive, we accepted an unconventional offer by the buyers. This is the scheme they concocted: If we accepted $40,000 in cash, we would record the sale of our house at a lower price, thereby paying less tax on the sale. It sounded good and we *stupidly* agreed. Of course, and as I've said, we were young, innocent, and trusting of everyone involved, and thus agreed to accept the balance of the funds in cash, but received nothing in writing.

As you may have guessed, the buyers decided to take advantage of the lower selling price, and conveniently forgot about the $40,000 in cash. "Our" lawyer informed us that they now expected to be able to pay $40,000 less than the original, agreed-upon price! This was not chump change, this was a disaster! We were frantic. On paper, the buyer was 100 percent in the right and the deal perfectly legal. To make matters worse, our lawyer explained that there was nothing he could do to help us!

Appealing to the buyers only made them angrier. They had us over a barrel financially, and this was not a time to add fuel to the fire! Calling our corrupt lawyer did no good. Purely by dumb luck, even though the papers had been drawn up, we had not yet signed them. We had, however, retained the lawyer at a cost of $800.

We had paid half the fee so far, and now decided that it was time to terminate his services.

Well, our lawyer would accept nothing of the kind. He was owed $400 and he had a solid case. He was in touch with the buyer and he stood to make money on the deal. (Who knows if those two parties had plans to split the $40,000?) We begged and pleaded for him to release us and return any paperwork, but he continuously and adamantly refused.

Our backs up against the wall, and having exhausted all legal means of dealing with the situation, we jokingly said we should get help from "someone with connections." It was the 1980s and Tony Soprano had not yet been created, but that was exactly who we needed! Luckily for us, we had an acquaintance who fit the bill. He looked like Tony Soprano, acted like Tony Soprano, and, most important of all, he agreed to come with us and use his powers of persuasion, specifically his intimidating looks, bulk, and brawn, to help us deal with our lawyer. He was flattered to have been approached, knowing that we looked up to him as both a savior and powerful ally.

And so it came to pass that the day of our appointment arrived and we entered the lawyer's office, armed with our reinforcement, however fake. It is a testament to our desperation that we felt compelled to pull off this sham in order to get out of our contract with the lawyer.

The first thing the lawyer said, nodding to our friend as we trooped into his office, was, "Who's this?" In a deep, threatening voice, our friend authoritatively responded to the question in one simple word: "Goombah." To this day, I don't know what it means, I don't even know for sure how to spell it, but it got the hoped-for response!

The lawyer was visibly shaken and asked us what we wanted. I proceeded to lace into him, my confidence buoyed by the presence of our intimidating friend, who was observing my tirade bemusedly and with newfound respect. Having prepared for a fight, the lawyer realized that this imposing presence was all that was necessary to change his position. I continued to admonish the lawyer, pointing out that we had paid him for a service that he had not provided satisfactorily, and we demanded to be immediately released from our contract with him. He nervously looked at our friend and said he'd see to it that the deal was off, but argued that we still had to pay him the $400 balance and he would not take a personal check.

The three of us quickly conferred, ran out and got a money order, then returned to the lawyer's office with all deliberate speed. We paid him and he handed over a folder of papers. We quickly left the office before we lost not only our advantage, but also our nerve. Standing outside on the sidewalk we were giddy with our success. What's $800 when we were previously facing a loss of $40,000? Our plan had worked! And all it had really taken was one little word, spoken by a hulking presence with an Italian accent.

We patted each other on the back in congratulations, and thanked our friend profusely for his part in our scheme. Being the modest man he was, he responded with, "You didn't need me; I can see you know how to handle yourselves just fine." Unceremoniously, he left.

As we stood there watching this commanding presence lumber away, we knew the truth. Whatever "Goombah" meant, we *absolutely* couldn't have done it without him!

SURVIVAL HINTS

1. You've heard it before: If something sounds too good to be true, it *is* too good to be true. Don't fall for underhanded schemes to save money. It will come back to haunt you.

2. Should you be crazy enough to try to break the law, be prepared for the consequences. Nothing good is ever gained illegally.

3. Avoid doing business with friends. But if you're foolish enough to do so, make sure to have your own enforcer around to intimidate them once they become your adversaries!

For Sale by Owner!

Ellen Steinberg

LAST YEAR I got it into my head to move. My kids were out of college and on their own, and my place was too big and too much work for me by myself. I wanted to move to a less suburban area, to a new life where there'd be other mature single professionals nearby. I'd been divorced for three years, and got the house in the settlement. Luckily that meant I didn't have to think about giving half the take to the cretin known as my ex-husband when the house was sold.

I also had heard so many ridiculous stories from my friends and relatives about Realtors who were useless, who let owners—after already cleaning, sprucing, and baking cookies for open houses—do all the work of actually showing the place too! On any occasion they were home, two of my sisters were each told, "Why don't you show them around—you know the place better than I do." Yet these folks still had their hands out for a hefty commission of anywhere from 3 to 6 percent of the selling price at the time of closing. This wasn't true of every Realtor, mind you, but my sisters had had bad experiences, and I wanted none of it. And so I became an expert at FSBO, or For Sale by Owner.

Selling your house yourself may sound simple, but it's not. It involves a lot of extra research and hard work, things that a good Realtor will do for you. For example, you need to find out the sale price of similar houses in your area. You can get this information in your local paper or, because it's a matter of public record, you can go down to the local courthouse and find the information there.

Not only that, but you need to place ads in all the appropriate newspapers. If you haven't done it yourself, you don't realize how time consuming and expensive this is. You pay by the word or the inch, depending on the newspaper, and you don't want to be too verbose because of the money involved, yet you can't be too terse or you won't attract buyers, especially when you're competing with the experts. I had to do my ad over because the first version just didn't cut it. But the second one, which was much more colorful and descriptive, generated a lot of drive-bys and calls for appointments, and that meant it was working.

Another thing you have to figure out yourself is what needs to be done to the place, inside and out. Now, some people who are addicted to house and garden TV shows could rattle off their items from a mental check-list, but those of us who would rather have bamboo wedged under our fingernails must really start from scratch. Outside I went from roof to curb and wrote down everything that seemed to need attention. This generated a new surface on the driveway, a new roof and paint job on the house, and fixing a broken window on the side of the garage. It was an expensive checklist but now the house looked great!

Inside I replaced a cracked sink in the powder room, had the carpets and furniture steam-cleaned, and had the kitchen painted a brighter, lighter color. I polished the wood cabinets myself, and went over the Italian tile floor with a special cleaner to make it sparkle. I also put softer, warmer bulbs in the bedroom lamps to give those rooms a more welcoming, relaxed feeling. It goes without saying that all clutter and paper has to be cleared away, and every single closet has to be neat and basically almost empty to give the impression of spacious storage areas. Same goes for the basement, attic, and garage.

At last I was done. Revised ads placed, I had my first open house. What a nightmare experience that was. I should have asked for some backup so that I wasn't alone with the first group that showed up. The open house was from 1 to 5 P.M. on a Sunday. Thirty people showed up, and as they wandered through the house, only some of them were supervised. Often those with small kids in tow did a lousy job of controlling them, leaving me with uprooted plants, broken vases, and spilled pitchers of cream on the coffee table. Never again! For the second open house, I had someone stationed in every room except the bathroom. This involved the forbearance of seven other people, who I then treated to dinner and a twenty-five-dollar gift certificate each from a local Starbucks.

Finally my first offer came. It was a lowball, $50,000 less than my asking price. Luckily a second offer came in for the full amount. Then came a third for almost the same amount. I was thrilled. But now I had to find out who was actually qualified to buy my house. This is when the real fun started. I asked for references and my lawyer examined all the paperwork. We had to run credit checks on the two better offers, rejected the third out of hand, and then they too came back with an improved offer—for the full asking price. By the time we'd gone through all the documents, we went to contract with the original people who'd made the lowball offer but came up.

Unfortunately, their mortgage company declined to approve the loan. Apparently the wife had lost her job a few months before, and in doing the calculation to approve the loan, the couple hadn't factored in the PMI, which is the mortgage insurance required if you put down less that 20 percent of the total price; they couldn't make their payments on just one salary. Not only that, but because it was a hot market, the finance company, despite advertising a no-points, no–closing costs deal, had also pulled back on that offer since the couple's finances weren't in pristine condition. Apparently they'd gotten behind on some bills lately, which led to a negative credit report. All of this contributed to the decision not to lend them the money.

By now I was beside myself because I'd put down a deposit on a condo in a great town that had a thriving downtown, and I'd even put in for a transfer so I'd be able to walk to work. But now I was back to square one. I was so frustrated that I started eating everything in sight, and before I knew it, I couldn't fit into my open house pants! I couldn't take it any more; I just wanted to get on with my life!

I called the other two interested parties. One had already gone to contract on another house, but the other was still looking. They came back and after haggling about the furnace, water heater, and laundry appliances—all of which were ten years old but worked just fine, but for which they wanted a discount on the price "just in case"—we sealed the deal. I found out later that a Realtor probably would have pooh-poohed that move, and it cost me about $2,000, but I was glad to have the negotiation completed.

We had a relatively smooth closing, thanks to my lawyer, who'd dealt with myriad FSBOs, and I was glad to be nearly done. Because my condo was still being built, I now was renting my own house for two months. The good thing about this was that I could pack in a leisurely fashion. The bad thing was that I actually had to give the new owner a security deposit of two months' rent to stay in my own house!

When the day came to move out, I swept the house clean per the contract, and the new owners came by to inspect the place. "Hmm," said the wife, "I don't remember these scuff marks on the wall in the hallway." And, "Oh, dear. What happened to our kitchen sink? It's all marked up with coffee stains." I reassured them that they'd all be taken care of, and I set about scouring and scrubbing. At last they handed me the check for my security deposit, minus $100 for "wear and tear." By this time I was in no mood for an argument, took the check, and drove off, never looking back.

When all was said and done and I figured out how much time I put into selling the house, I estimated that I spent about twenty hours a week for three months. It was like an unpaid part-time job. But, when I factored in the savings on the commission I would have paid, I came out so far ahead that it really was worth it in my case.

My aunt asked me the other day if I'd do another FSBO in the future. Honestly, it would depend on the circumstances and my finances, but probably not. I'm glad I did it, and I think it turned out well, but it really takes *a lot* of extra time and effort. I'd rather spend the time enjoying life instead, next time around!

SURVIVAL HINTS

1. If it's a hot real estate market and you decide to have open houses, be sure to have enough friends or family as backup to escort the "viewers."
2. If you can write clever ad copy, then go for it!
3. If you're too busy to handle all the details yourself, you'd be better off opting for a Realtor.

Filthy Rich?

Gina Jacobs

STRESSFUL DOESN'T EVEN begin to describe the home-selling experience. Home buying is no walk in the park either, but sellers are the ones in the spotlight.

I've moved several times in my thirty-something years. Each time I think I've reached my final destination, I inevitably find myself giving my house a one-coat paint-lift, scurrying to pick up the eternal mess, and packing my life's possessions into boxes. Just in case my own traumas of selling weren't enough, a few years ago I became a Realtor. So now I witness firsthand the pain and suffering of others.

As a seller, you want a fairly quick sale. That is, unless you enjoy trying to keep your house spotless every moment of every day! I don't claim to be a guru on cleanliness but

I have certainly seen enough homes to offer a little insight for those without a clue. Just because you offer your house for sale does not make your house salable. Being salable means being tidy. Once you get your house tidy, *it must stay that way until it sells!* I promise you that the day you head out for work leaving dirty dishes in the sink, breakfast crumbs on the floor, and all the beds unmade, you will come home to find a real state agent showing your house. You will wish you hadn't come home at all! At least then these strangers in your home wouldn't be able to put a face with the mess that surrounds them. It's embarrassing to be caught *dirty*. As a mother of two mess-attracting, clutter-creating boys, I thought I knew dirty. I was wrong.

Selling real estate for several years now, I've learned that every house is unique, just like the people who live there. I was showing a house recently that was being sold "as is." That's real-estate-ese for "expect the worst so you won't be disappointed."

As I brought my well-dressed buyer client through the front door, he and I were stopped dead in our tracks. The stench of cat urine almost knocked us backwards! The smell was so bad our eyes were burning! But that was a good thing because it forced us to squint, which means we didn't have to clearly see the other surprises this house had to offer. We pressed on through the front door into the stink. Unmade beds and dirty dishes would have been a welcome sight by comparison. This house had bare mattresses on the floor and the dirty dishes were certainly not limited to the sink, or even to just the kitchen for that matter.

Partially eaten food was strewn throughout the house. We discovered chicken bones and partially consumed pudding-snack cups on the floor and pizza crust on the dresser. This wasn't just breakfast crumbs! This house hadn't been cleaned since the Last Supper and part of *that* supper was still here on the floor!

My client handled it well, perhaps better than I did. He wanted an investment property, so here we were. Surely, the value of this house would increase the minute the pigs left the sty—er, *I mean*, as soon as the sellers vacated the premises.

Just when I thought it couldn't get any worse, we ventured into the basement. Unfinished basements are rarely pretty and they are my least favorite area of any dwelling. The basement in this house was obviously the feline hub, as was evident by the multiple dirty litter boxes, soiled cat toys, and cat feces on the cold cement floor.

If that wasn't enough, the unrecognizable dead cat prey I nearly stepped on was a considerable shock. There it was, only inches from my treasured Kenneth Cole black suede pumps. It was bloodied and ripped apart. Only a few remaining mangled feathers identified it as a bird. *And that concludes our tour . . .* , I thought to myself. A squeamish grin exchanged with my client and we were out the door!

My client did not buy that house but it did eventually sell, months later and for about $25,000 less than the original asking price! Proof positive that there *really* is a buyer for every house.

The moral of the story here is that cleanliness can only *help* your sale, while the lack of it can be extremely damaging. There are undoubtedly varying degrees of cleanliness but it's a virtue that is achievable by *everyone*. Sellers, if you won't tidy up for yourself, at least do it for the unsuspecting potential buyers and definitely for your real estate agents! I don't think I ever would have fully recovered had I actually stepped on that decomposing bird carcass!

SURVIVAL HINTS

1. Pick up every time you leave your house for the duration of the listing period. You *never* know when your buyer is going to walk through the door.
2. Burn scented candles often to disguise pet smells. Your nose may be accustomed to those familiar smells, but others will be more sensitive to odors such as pets and cigarette smoke.
3. If you have dead animals in your home, it might be time to clean!

6

When You'll Try Anything to Unload It

St. Joseph, Sales Agent
Evelyn M. Fazio

Chuckie
Helene Ellis

Packaging Reality
Carole A. Daley

The Nightmare Tenant
Joan Morath

Fixing It Up to Sell
Tom Philbin

A Little Paint Can Mean Big Money
Pete Ross

The Suspicious Closing
Joe Beck

Sanity Quiz

You just can't understand it. Your house has been on the market for over a year and you haven't had a single bite. Other houses in your area are selling briskly right and left, but yours is at a virtual standstill. Of course the exterior paint is peeling a little but it's not bad, the lawn looks a little dried out but with a little effort it could be great. As you sit back and watch, the house next door sells. You can't believe it! The neighbors' house is half the size of yours, and sold for your asking price.

Do you
A. ask them what their secret is
B. lower your asking price
C. stay put and forget about selling the damn thing
D. put a little work and effort into the place and get your sale quickly

No matter how you answered the question, read on and see what techniques our contributors tried—it's just about everything you can think of!

St. Joseph, Sales Agent

Evelyn M. Fazio

SOMETIMES PEOPLE NEED a little extra help selling their homes, and sometimes their methods can be a little unconventional. Apparently, some of that extra help can come from St. Joseph, the patron saint of carpenters. Or at least his statue can help, but you have to bury it upside down in the yard of your house that you're having trouble selling. No, I'm not kidding. And I found out that it's not only crazy Italians who do this.

When I was working in Westchester County, in New York State, my friend, who is Scandinavian, was having a hard time selling her home in nearby Connecticut. The house, which was beautiful and in a prime neighborhood with huge wooded lots, had been on the market for quite a while, a lot longer than anyone expected. By now it was almost two years, and it was holding up the couple's plans to retire and move upstate to a house in the country.

That's when I first heard of this business about the statue of St. Joseph. Someone told my friend, who by now was quite frustrated, that this statue technique always worked, even if you weren't Catholic. Sounded goofy to me, but what do I know?

Next thing I heard, the statue was planted upside down in her yard, per the custom—and less than a month later, there was an offer on the house! And then a second one! Hmmm. I wondered if this was just a result of the amount of time involved—something had to give eventually, didn't it?

I pretty much forgot about that whole episode, that is, until another St. Joseph story surfaced. This time, it was a local house in the town where I live. The seller was my aunt, who really wanted to sell her house and move to senior citizen housing where she wouldn't have to shovel snow, rake leaves, or worry about a house as she got older. She was much more interested in playing bingo, going to Atlantic City to gamble, or spending time with her grandchildren and her friends. But her house wasn't moving. Things were dragging along, when one of her friends told her about burying St. Joseph. Soon my aunt got a statue from her Realtor, then planted it as directed, head first into the ground—poor guy! It all seemed so rude.

Wouldn't you know it, a developer happened along and decided that a group of four houses located on a desirable corner in town—close to bus lines, the major university medical center, and easy access to local highways—would be the ideal spot for a townhouse development. My aunt and her neighbors got premium prices for their houses, and away they went. The houses were demolished, the townhouses went up, and everyone was happy. St. Joseph got dug up, of course, and was on his way to his next assignment.

The final example of St. Joseph's statue's good effects involves my cousin and his lovingly restored house with beautiful rosebushes in bloom and a bountiful garden in the backyard. Despite the meticulous condition of his house, it just wouldn't sell. He had a part-time Realtor who only showed the house on weekends—unless it rained or she was busy doing something else. At this rate, the house was going to end up on the market well into the next millennium.

Then a good friend of the family told my cousin about the St. Joseph statue. Another friend offered to lend him hers, and into the ground went St. Joseph. Suddenly, a family took interest in the house and made an offer that was readily accepted. It only took a week. St. Joseph strikes again!

By this point, all the talk about St. Joseph and his real estate prowess made me curious, so I did a little research. As you may already know, St. Joseph is the patron saint of workers in addition to carpenters. He's the foster father of Jesus, husband of Mary, and a carpenter by trade. Maybe his carpentry background is the connection to people relying on his help in selling a house, since houses were usually made of wood.

There are several different legends that involve calling on St. Joseph for help in procuring land with good results for whoever made the request. But there seems to be more than one basis for the practice of burying the statues. One story involves nuns in the Middle Ages burying a religious medal of St. Joseph to help them get their own convent on that exact spot, and another recounts a story of a nineteenth-century monk burying a St. Joseph medal in the ground he wanted to acquire for his monastery. In both cases, there were claims of success. But what made them bury a St. Joseph's medal as opposed to some other saint? What made them bury it rather than place it on a rock or pedestal? Who knows? There's also speculation that the legend may stem from German carpenters' tradition of leaving statues of St. Joseph in the foundations of the houses they built. It's possible, but maybe today's statue-burying has nothing to do with any of this.

Whatever the origins of the tradition, there are now lots of sources for the statues. One store in Chicago sells thirty to fifty of the little plastic statues every week to people from all sorts of religious backgrounds who want to sell their houses. So it's not just a quirky local East Coast practice, which I had expected. There's even a company that sells several versions of St. Joseph home sale kits, complete with statues, prayer cards, and other components. And if that's not enough, there's a Web site that offers these St. Joseph kits in bundles of five, ten, and twenty, specifically for sale to Realtors for their clients. You can even find the kits in Spanish! I also found out that for sellers who live in condos or co-ops, apparently the little statue can be buried just as effectively in a flowerpot—it's supposed to work as well as planting it outside a house. It's a strange world indeed.

Now I don't know if any of this is coincidence, voodoo, or what, but if I ever have trouble selling, I know what I'm going to do!

Chuckie

Helene Ellis

WE WERE SELLING our house, and Chuckie was caus-
ing us trouble. We called him Chuckie, in spite of our
resistance to give the little bugger a name. He was the
offspring of the woodchuck family we observed out the
kitchen window on the east slope of our twenty acres.
Deer, dog, kids, pheasants, turkeys, rabbits—we all lived
together on this charming piece of land in rural southern Michigan. The motion-detector light had been
sufficient to keep the big animals away from the orna-
mental bushes around the house. The little ones were
never really a nuisance, doing a little ground-level trimming and going back to their own burrows far away
from us.

One morning as we were preparing to show the
house to prospective buyers we noticed a huge mound

of earth at the edge of the porch near a holly bush. A closer look showed the dark hole with a tunnel going down under the porch cement pad. A woodchuck! The mound, with its fluff of newly dug soil and disturbed spiders and beetles standing around quizzically trying to figure out what happened to their own little abodes, did not fit into our carefully orchestrated first impression or "curb appeal."

Prospective buyers were coming in a few days. We had to do *something* to discourage Chuckie from building under our porch. First we filled in the hole, organizing several rocks in a pleasing display. We bought a few creeping Texas roses to drape over the rocks. Apparently Chuckie didn't like the ambience, or maybe the fact that we destroyed his portal. By morning he had completed another mound, spewing dirt all over the rocks we had so carefully decorated.

Next we bought a forty-dollar live trap and placed it on the path leading to the porch. Then we tried to entice Chuckie with lettuce and broccoli in a gourmet presentation. He took the bait, but not in the trap.

So. This is how it's going to be. Okay, you little bastard (we submitted to primal territorial frustration), take this! We stuffed the garden hose down the hole and let it run for awhile until we wondered if such a tactic might have an effect on the foundation of the porch. Every battle plan had to be executed without destroying the very house we built. Chuckie returned.

Then we sprayed every pest repellent we could find, including something called coyote urine (how they ever got the stuff I don't want to know). No luck. Still Chuck.

We then buried empty long-neck beer bottles surrounding his doorway to scare him away when the bottles clanked together (something we have heard worked—we wouldn't have thought of *that* on our own). We found the opposite entrance on the wood side of the porch and did the same there. Still Chuckie simply removed any disturbing items we sent down the hole or left at his doorways.

Time was running out. We had buyers coming the next day. Every other aspect of our exhausting preparations were in place—new drapes, clean windows, we'd installed the French doors we always said we would put up leading from the bedroom to the porch. It was beautiful, except for the "resident" below.

We tried ground glass. We broke a bottle and, wearing heavy work gloves, we carefully threw the glass down into the holes of Chuckie's house. Mean, yes, I admit it, but we were desperate! We primed the little rock garden, covered Chuckie's mound with decorative stone and congratulated ourselves on our creativity.

The next morning we took a deep breath, hoping that a mutilated fur body did not lie outside the porch. Instead, we were shocked into a deep respect for what we had previously considered a lowly animal on the intellectual hierarchy of mammals. During the night, Chuckie had dug his way out of the portal, kicking the decorative stones in all directions and carefully lining up the broken glass outside his door. We were defeated by a stronger will.

When the prospective buyers came, we hoped they wouldn't notice the covered evidence of Chuckie's life with us. But to our surprise, one of the buyers said, "Oh, I see you have a woodchuck too." A round of stories followed in the good spirit of living in the country.

SURVIVAL HINTS

1. If you want to live in the country, expect to share it with "nature."
2. If you have a woodchuck, get used to it, or call a professional wildlife removal service. These animals are smarter than you think.
3. Don't be surprised by anything your local fauna come up with to outwit you!

Packaging Reality

Carole A. Daley

OVER THE COURSE of our marriage, Jim and I have moved numerous times. Job promotions, coma-inducing commutes, unleashed dogs, neighbors that "loved too much," or neighbors that "loved too little," kept us moving from one end of California to the other. I've been skunked a couple of times; but overall the changes have been welcomed.

We were living in the heat of central California (one of the times I got skunked) when an opportunity arose to relocate back to the coast. The dim yet pleasant memory of a simpler time spent in Marin County—before kids, pets, and mortgages—drew us back just north of the Golden Gate Bridge. Finding the perfect house was easy, too easy as it turned out. Never mind that it seemed cheap by Bay Area standards and had been on the market, empty, for over a year. Ignoring the fact that our Realtor's office was just one block away from this gem, and he hadn't mentioned the house to us, we grabbed it, no questions asked.

Atop a steep driveway the house stood four stories tall—garage on the ground floor, three flights of stairs to the front door and guest quarters, another flight to the kitchen and living rooms, and two more short flights of stairs to the bedrooms. The result of all this stair-climbing was commanding views of the bay and the scenic little town. Alas, no elevator, no dumbwaiter—just dumb owners. The mere act of grocery shopping took on a whole new meaning.

Three years later, facilitated by yet another job promotion, it was time to move on. We knew that unless we could find an athletic buyer looking for a gigantic piece of workout equipment moonlighting as a home, we were in for a long selling period.

Olga was the third Realtor we interviewed. Her tall, thin frame and tightly pulled back black hair made me wonder if she had given up a career as a prima ballerina to be a real estate agent. Except for her hair, she was a picture in beige from her cashmere pantsuit and buttery soft shoes to her flawless, antique Mercedes convertible.

We timidly inquired about the negative impact the stairs might have on the sale. "Stairs?" she whispered with disdain. "A little exercise never hurt anyone. Besides, when we get through with this place, no one will think about the stairs." Jim and I signed up on the spot, and soon found out that "We" meant her color consultant, painter, floor refinisher, and staging person. But her estimate of the time and cost of "getting top dollar" seemed reasonable to us. Besides, she was willing to oversee all the work.

Because Jim's promotion had been sudden, and we'd booked and paid for a vacation eight time zones away, Olga encouraged us to go. It would leave her with no messy clients underfoot while she tidied the place up a bit.

About halfway through our vacation, Olga faxed us with a simple command: "Call me ASAP." Via transatlantic call, Jim discovered Olga's initial estimate of tidying-up costs had been low. He balked at Olga's request for more funds. Not to be deterred, Olga tossed in a line: "Let me tell you a story. I could buy a three-dollar lipstick at the corner drugstore, but I buy lipstick that costs thirty dollars a tube. Do you know why?"

Jim took the bait, "Why?"

Olga set the hook, "Because the packaging and advertising promises me perfection." So Olga continued to package our house.

We returned from vacation to gleaming wood floors, towering lush plants, freshly painted walls, and scaled-down furniture. Our oversized, overstuffed furniture was nowhere to be seen. "Your furniture," Olga announced with a dismissive wave of her manicured hand, "is in storage."

The rented furniture fit the narrow spaces of our four-story treehouse perfectly. Everything looked so good that we were tempted to keep the house—until we tried living in it. The chairs were hard and unforgiving; the table nestled into the small, awkward space of the kitchen was, well, awkward. Replacing our king-sized bed with a double bed magically transformed our cramped bedroom into a master suite, but left us with limited sleeping space.

And Olga wasn't finished with her magic. The subsequent open houses and individual showings featured perfect temperatures, soothing yet sophisticated music, and abundant floral displays (memories of Olga's magic probably account for the fact that the next three houses we bought were void of occupants, furniture, and aural delights).

I tried to do my part to keep up the illusion of perfection. When Olga called to warn me of a showing, I would scoop up our two small terriers and stuff them into my car where water and food awaited their hyperactive presence. In the kitchen, dog bowls and beds were shoved unceremoniously into a cupboard.

I became obsessed with toilet paper. Each holder had to have a plump, snowy white, unused roll. Maybe luxurious TP was just the subliminal message needed to minimize the endless stairs. I decided that nothing says "You belong here" as well as toilet paper.

Olga cautioned it would be best if we were out of the house whenever an interested party was on the scene.

However, late one afternoon Olga broke her own rule. She called to say a potential buyer and her friend were sitting in front of the house perusing the flyer taken from the box I dutifully filled several times a day. Olga was miles away and the women didn't have a Realtor. "Could you show them the house?" Olga queried, then added, "It's probably a waste of time, but it's up to you."

Of course I acquiesced, and with no time to stuff the dogs into my car unobserved, or refresh the toilet paper, I hiked down to the bottom of the hill and invited them up. I was careful to spring lightly up the steep stairway to give the illusion that it was nothing to climb these steps, perhaps several times a day. Not to be outdone, the women followed my lead. They were panting heavily by the time we topped the stairs, while I willed myself to breathe quietly.

On that initial visit, the two ladies never got further than the floor-to-ceiling picture windows and the expansive views. The potential buyer's husband had recently left her and She Who Had Been Forsaken was visiting from the Midwest. Her friend lived in San Francisco and thought looking at real estate might cheer up Forsaken. The gods were smiling on me that day. Forsaken's soon-to-be-ex had very deep pockets and Forsaken had a very good lawyer. Our sparkling home with its romantic views was just what Forsaken thought she needed.

Her only reservation about the house was the suitability for her little bedroom slipper of a dog. I'm not sure it actually had eyes—I never saw them. The presence of my neurotic pets did the trick. I showed her the yard—a tiny dark patio.

Forsaken bought the house, closed within the month (all cash), put in a doggie door to "the yard," promptly rearranged the interior walls, moved her grand piano by crane to the second floor, and resold the house within the year. We suspect her decision to sell arose from her discovery that it was impossible to install an elevator.

Buying and selling homes is a messy human business, guaranteed to age you ten years in the space of a few weeks even if the market isn't sliding south and you aren't wrenching children from their schools and friends. On the other hand, you'll be amazed by what you can accomplish when you're motivated to make that sale!

SURVIVAL HINTS

1. Clean sells. When buying it's "location, location, location," but when selling it's "clean, clean, clean."

2. Pick the right agent. I interviewed three agents. There are plenty to choose from, so choose one with whom you are compatible.

3. The listing price. After asking the agent for all the comparable homes for sale or recently sold in my area, I drive by the properties. Taking a stab at what I think my home is worth can expose a Realtor who is throwing out a high number just to get the listing.

4. You need only one buyer. It doesn't matter what *usually* works for the agent. Realtors love to talk about the statistics of home buying and selling. But we don't need to know how most homes are bought and sold or what rarely works. You only need one buyer as soon as possible.

5. Insist on open houses every Saturday or Sunday. And keep a pile of persuasive handouts to keep the flyer box full and easily accessible to any Realtor willing to show the home to a potential buyer, day or night.

6. Dear buyer, picture yourself here. I try to keep my personality and bad taste out of sight. I rent furniture when mine just doesn't make the cut. I hire people to remind me that living rooms shouldn't look like home offices. First impressions do count.

The Nightmare Tenant

Joan Morath

MY HUSBAND AND I had built a beautiful home on a huge lot in Allendale, New Jersey, back before New Jersey became the overcrowded state it is today. We had a booming business and our lives were comfortable. But as time went on the town had grown and our large property was now surrounded by other homes. Our initial attraction to this area had been space—something that we now were losing and at an uncomfortably quick rate. After several discussions we decided it was time to move on to a less crowded, congested area where we could have more land and fewer neighbors.

Not waiting for the sale of our house, we found and purchased one further north and made the move immediately. After putting the first house on the market, we decided we would try our hands at being landlords. Why not, it's better than leaving the house empty while awaiting a sale—or so we thought.

This was our first experience with a tenant. We were very much in the dark, and unprepared for the battles we were about to face. First, the renter was a pack rat. He kept everything from old newspapers to garbage to half-eaten food thrown about the house. Not only that but on many occasions he refused entry to the Realtor who was trying to sell our house. Not that anyone would have purchased it in the messy condition he'd created, so his reluctance turned out to be a blessing. I would have died if he'd let anyone into the house given the mess he'd made of it.

He caused problem after problem, including damaging the house. He put large holes in the walls, burnt the carpet in several spots, broke windows—you name it. He was a landlord's worst nightmare.

We realized that if the sale was ever going to happen we would first need to evict him. Well, that was easier said than done. He refused to leave, stopped paying his rent altogether, and continued to destroy the house. If you've never tried to evict someone, the process is both time consuming and costly. It took us a little over a year to get him out, all the while never receiving one red cent of rent that he owed us. The eviction process ended up costing us additional attorney fees. The end result wasn't pretty: He had to be forcibly removed by the police.

The combined expense of the eviction and returning our house to its previous state ended up in the high tens of thousands of dollars, all of which came out of our pocket. It took us three additional months after the eviction for the repairs to be completed and the house put back on the market. Then it sold within the first week. We never recouped the damages from the deadbeat, and I learned two things: Being a landlord is not for everyone, and it's also not a great idea to rent out your house while you're trying to sell it unless you're certain that your tenant is a neat freak.

SURVIVAL HINTS

1. If you plan to rent your home while waiting for a sale, be sure to fully check out your prospective tenants. I recommend asking for references— some personal but not family, and two from previous landlords. Business references can also provide good character references. If possible, a credit check can also help ensure that your prospective tenant pays his bills.

2. Being a landlord is a complicated process. Make sure you research it fully so you know and understand your rights. Get legal counsel prior to making this decision. You don't want to be sorry later.

3. Ask your Realtor for an estimate for how long it's going to take to sell your home. Then weigh your options. If he or she expects a sale within the first year, renting is definitely not worth the time or trouble.

Fixing It Up to Sell

Tom Philbin

AS A HOME-IMPROVEMENT expert and author of several books, I am often asked about fixer-uppers and how a homeowner can best protect himself when working with a contractor. The best answer is: money is the most important thing. And the bottom line is this: As long as you never let the contractor get ahead of you on the money, you can't get burned. If he has money in his pocket for work not yet done, then you can get scorched.

One story sticks in my mind that illustrates the power of money in dealing contractors. During a question-and-answer session after one of my library talks, a lady stood up and talked about the power of money when handling contractors.

"I was getting my house ready to be sold," she said, "and while it was in a pretty good shape, the kids' bathroom was a disaster. It not only needed new tile and a new sink, bath, and tub, but it also needed work on the pipes. We figured we had to do it. If we didn't, prospective buyers would be turned off."

She went on: "We hired a contractor named Tony to do the work. He did a pretty nice job, and he did it fairly quickly. But before he left—I didn't know any better—I gave him the final payment of a couple of thousand dollars.

"Later that same night, I was down in the basement and heard a sound that made it seem like little fishies were swimming in my stomach. I investigated and realized that my original suspicion was right. The water was coming from the remodeled bath.

"In a panic, I called Tony and told him about the water. "'Can you come back and fix it?'

"'No problem,' Tony said. 'No problem at all.'

"'So what time will you be here tomorrow?'

"'Oh,' Tony said, 'I can't make it tomorrow.'

"'When can you make it?'

"'In about a month.'

"'But,' I gasped, '*I have water running inside my walls.*'

"'I'm sorry,' Tony said, 'it's the best I can do.'

"An idea came to me. 'Okay, Tony,' I said, 'tomorrow morning I'll be at the bank at 9 A.M. stopping payment on that two-thousand-dollar check I gave you today.'

"So the next morning, guess where Tony was at 8 A.M.? At my house fixing the leak."

Why did this work out so well for her? Because she followed the rules of money and contractors. In case you're not familiar with them, here are the three money rules people need know to protect themselves with contractors:

1. They should never give an advance for materials— except on custom jobs where material can't be returned.
2. The payments should be staggered so that only work that is completed is paid for.
3. At the end of the job, some money should be held out for a couple of weeks until the job settles. This way you can see that when it rains the roof doesn't leak.

All turned out well for the lady from the library. Had she not had the savvy to stop the funds on this contractor, she might be swimming through her house—or what would have been left of it—after the water damage had run its course. It's just like I said, when you're dealing with contractors, money *is* the most important thing!

A Little Paint Can Mean Big Money

Pete Ross

I KNOW FROM firsthand experience that painting your home before putting it on the market can mean a significant increase in good offers. The first house I sold was on the market for four years. People came and looked, but they never came back. It just didn't seem to have the same appeal as when I'd first bought it twenty years before.

The years had certainly taken their toll. The paint on the exterior of the house was chipped and peeling. The interior paint was dark and dingy, and, to be perfectly honest, the overall effect was kind of unwelcoming. I initially figured, *Why put the time and money into making this place look better when I was moving out?* But at this rate the house wasn't selling, even at a low asking price for our area. Things were at a standstill: four years and not one offer. I was getting nowhere.

One day while standing on the sidewalk comparing my house to my neighbors on the right and the left, I finally saw what my prospective buyers had been seeing all along: an old eyesore of a house. Both the houses on either side of mine were ten years younger and both had been repainted recently. I could now see why someone would want to skip right on past mine and go on to the next. In fact, if I were a prospective buyer, I probably would have done the same thing. My house just wasn't up to par.

That's when I finally decided that, if I ever wanted to move out, I had to do something, and fast. By far the easiest and cheapest face-lift for a home is a paint job. It's also something you can sometimes do yourself. After all was said and done, it took me about two weeks to do both the interior and exterior of the house, but what a huge difference it finally made. It took years off its life. The house looked nearly brand new again, and not only did it blend in with my neighbors' beautiful homes, it looked better than both of them.

About a week after the paint job, a new Realtor came to reevaluate the house. In consultation with the Realtor, we upped the asking price by $30,000, and back on the market it went. In less than two weeks, we not only received a bid for the full asking price, but three other bids above our price as well. With just a little bit of paint and some sweat on my part, the house ended up selling for $42,000 more than I originally asked. What a difference a little paint can make!

The Suspicious Closing

Joe Beck

MY FRIEND SCOTT is a thirty-year-veteran real-estate
lawyer from Virginia. He's represented buyers and sellers in hundreds of transactions during his career, and
also teaches real-estate law at the college level. He tells
me that not all home sales or purchases drive the buyer
or seller crazy. In some cases, it's the real estate lawyer
who can suffer. Here's a story he told me about a closing
that illustrates the point.

"Most closings are fairly routine, but of all those I've
handled, there's one I'll never forget. My secretary set a
time and date for a routine closing. It was to be a typical
transaction, with both the buyer and the seller repre-
senting their elderly mothers. But at the appointed time
and date, nobody showed up. I waited at the office for
another hour and finally left for the night.

"Two days later the buyer showed up at my office, unannounced. I was taken aback because the person didn't seem to be aware of how inappropriate it was to have skipped the closing without as much as a phone call to postpone, only to show up on a different day without an appointment.

"'Sir,' I explained, 'at a real-estate closing you need to have certain documents and monies available to complete the transaction.'

"'Sure, no problem,' the man said.

"'Well, you're here and you don't know how much money you need for the closing fees. I haven't disclosed them to you. Are you sure you're ready?' I asked.

"'That's no problem. I always come prepared,' the man replied. With that, he stood up and reached into his coat pocket and pulled out a plastic shopping bag full of twenty-dollar bills. He proceeded to count out $8,000 in twenties.

"Stunned, I looked at the man. 'Sir, I have to be honest with you. In many years of practicing law, I've never seen anything like this before. Do you always carry this much cash around with you? Where did you get all this money?' I was naturally suspicious, and something about this cash bothered me.

"'I own several gas stations and customers pay us with twenty-dollar bills.' I took the money and immediately had my secretary deposit it in the bank. It was under the $10,000 legal limit required to notify the IRS of a cash deposit, and I didn't want that much cash lying around the office. Now all that remained was to reschedule the closing and fill out the remaining paperwork.

"A few days before the new closing date, I called the buyer and seller to verify the appointment, to remind them of the documents they needed, and to tell both parties to bring their mothers to sign the documents. I was told the mothers might not be there, as they were elderly and had limited mobility. The day before the closing, I received a call from the buyer, and I again reminded him that his mother must be there. I was told she'd do her best to make it.

"Finally, on the morning of the rescheduled closing, something told me to call the buyer and seller one more time to insist that both mothers appear. The closing couldn't happen without them because their names were on the deeds.

"Then the buyer dropped the bomb: 'What if the mothers don't exist? What would happen then?' he asked. By now, I had had enough. I told the buyer to return to my office on the next business day and I would have a certified bank check waiting for him in the amount of $8,000—the original cash deposit. The man showed up, apologized for the confusion, accepted the check, and left. I was glad to put the incident behind me and be rid of this peculiar buyer.

"About two months later, I received a subpoena from the FBI. When I called the FBI, I was asked why I had written a check to that individual for $8,000. I explained that it was the deposit I had returned to the man, and that I was relieved to be done with him. The FBI agent then informed me that the man in question was a major drug kingpin who had concocted a phony real-estate scam (with fictitious elderly mothers!) to launder his illegal drug money—this time in the amount of $8,000. The bank check he received from me for his refunded deposit was now considered 'clean.'

"The drug kingpin in question was now being held without bail for trial, said the FBI agent, and I might be called on to testify against him. But as it turned out, I wasn't subpoenaed. It was just as well. With all the honest closings I had scheduled, I didn't need to be wasting time in court!"

SURVIVAL HINTS

1. If your buyer or seller is asking for something unreasonable, ask questions.
2. If it doesn't feel right, be careful. Sometimes your gut instincts can save you an awful lot of trouble.
3. Watch out for scams and unethical behavior— they can come back to haunt you!

Acknowledgments

The authors would like to thank all our contributors, especially Susan Berlin, Carole A. Daley, P. J. Dempsey, Ray Zardetto, Kyle Ezell, Ginny Chandoha, Bob Toriello, and Arline Simpson, all of whom wrote for other Staying Sane volumes. We also welcome newcomers Helene Ellis, Gina Jacobs, Tom Miller, Bill Coughlin, Brian Craig, George Primov, Tom Prichard, and Tom Philbin.